THE ELEMENTS OF ORCHESTRATION

THE ELEMENTS OF ORCHESTRATION

By

GORDON JACOB
D.Mus., F.R.C.M., Hon. R.A.M.

GREENWOOD PRESS, PUBLISHERS
WESTPORT, CONNECTICUT

Library of Congress Cataloging in Publication Data

Jacob, Gordon Percival Septimus, 1895-
    The elements of orchestration.

    Reprint of the 1962 ed. published by H. Jenkins,
London.
    Bibliography: p.
    Includes index.
    1. Instrumentation and orchestration. I. Title.
[MT70.J18 1976]   781.6'4   76-15191
ISBN 0-8371-8955-1

© GORDON JACOB 1962
All rights reserved

First published in 1962 by Herbert Jenkins, London

Reprinted with the permission of Barrie & Jenkins

Reprinted in 1976 by Greenwood Press,
a division of Williamhouse-Regency Inc.

Library of Congress Catalog Card Number 76-15191

ISBN 0-8371-8955-1

Printed in the United States of America

CONTENTS

6

ACKNOWLEDGMENTS

The author offers thanks for permission to quote from copyright works as follows:

Messrs. Boosey and Hawkes	Ex. 5, 9 Moussorgsky-Ravel "Pictures from an Exhibition"
Messrs. Boosey and Hawkes	Ex. 17 Bartok, "Concerto for Orchestra"
Messrs. Brietkopf and Härtel (Leipzig)	Ex. 20 Sibelius, Symphony No. 1
British and Continental Music Agency Ltd.	Ex. 41 Elgar, Organ Sonata in G.

FOREWORD

IN MUSIC more than any of the arts proficiency can only be gained by the close study of other men's work. Especially is this true of the creative side of music making. Such study is not for the purpose of learning a few tricks and gestures so as to be able to reproduce them at second hand, but is undertaken as a means of acquiring ease in handling the basic materials and knowledge of what has already been done as a foundation on which to build a style of one's own. If originality is there the study of masterpieces, far from injuring it, will stimulate and encourage invention. The artist may admire many of his illustrious predecessors and contemporaries and may love their work. But he will not show these feelings by imitating their styles but by striving to come near to their spirit of adventure and independence of thought in his own work. Composition in all its branches is not to be compared with any sister art. Painting and drawing come naturally to children and their efforts in that direction are rightly admired though later study often takes away the bloom of spontaneity. Writing is a skill which, though there is much to be learned about it, can be practised by any educated person because its raw materials are the words of everyday usage. But music is highly artificial in the old sense of the word, at any rate in its more sophisticated manifestations, and though there are " composers " who cannot read or write music but have a knack of turning out catchy tunes, they have to rely on the help of musical craftsmen to give their ideas convincing expression and acceptable professional accoutrements.

In this book, as its title shows, there is no attempt to deal with the complicated processes of composition and orchestration employed by progressive composers today. Originality is obviously

9

synonymous with unconventionality and departure from or modification of traditional material. But you cannot depart from or modify material unless you are thoroughly conversant with it, and if I have succeeded in convincing my readers of the necessity for grasping the essential principles of orchestration by going to the works of the great masters of the art, my purpose will have been fulfilled.

I have not dealt with the problems of arranging keyboard music for orchestra because that is the basis of teaching which I have set out in my manual *Orchestral Technique* (Oxford University Press). Similarly score-reading is treated more fully than it is here in my little book *How to Read a Score* (Boosey & Hawkes Ltd.).

I have given the compasses of the instruments and a few remarks about them in the last chapter of this book so that they can be easily looked up, but I am writing here specifically on the subject of orchestration, and full information concerning the individual instruments and their technique can be obtained from the text-books whose titles I have given in a short bibliography at the end.

G. J.

Saffron Walden, Essex.

PART I
THEORY

CHAPTER I

AN OUTLINE OF THE HISTORY OF ORCHESTRATION
FROM HAYDN TO THE PRESENT DAY

THE ART of orchestration, as it is understood today, may be said to date from the second half of the eighteenth century, at which time something like a settled constitution of the orchestra began to be established.

Before that time composers worked to a great extent in isolation and were obliged to make use of such instruments as were available locally. The contrapuntal nature of their music also precluded much in the way of the massive effects achieved by block harmony, and the chief requisite was that the linear strands should be roughly of equal strength. This does not mean that the orchestration of such composers as Bach and Handel was crude or haphazard, but to them music was a texture of sounds in which instrumental colour did not play such an important part as the contrapuntal pattern resulting from the interplay of parts or " voices " regardless of the actual instruments they were played upon. In the matter of instrumental obbligati such as we find in the B minor Mass of Bach there is much evidence to show that the characters of different instruments were fully appreciated and differentiated in the composer's mind, but his orchestra as a whole was treated as a large chamber-music combination. The changing style of musical composition from polyphony to homophony was accompanied by, and indeed required, a more solid and settled structure for the orchestra. It must be remembered that this change was not abrupt. Many die-hard composers went on in the old ways long past the middle of the eighteenth century, disregarding the work of the more pioneering

13

spirits who had begun to experiment with the new methods of composition quite early in that century. The orchestra had also to free itself from the thrall of the continuo which had been a necessary cohesive and stabilising background to the contrapuntal activity of the other instruments but which naturally tended to stand in the way of vivid contrasts of tone-colour by its unwearying insistence. In actual fact the " conductor at the piano " lasted well into the nineteenth century long after he had ceased either to play or conduct. Until baton-conducting became established as the regular thing custom ordained that there should be somewhere on the platform a man seated at a keyboard, the principal violinist being the real " concert-master " or conductor.

When the baton-conductor in his turn wrested the power from the principal violin the latter still retained the position of importance which survives today. The " leader ", as he is now called, has to be prepared to deputise for the conductor, and acts as a liaison between him and the orchestra. He therefore has to be a man of outstanding personal qualifications whom his colleagues can respect both as a musician and a man, and who can adapt himself to all sorts of conditions of conductors—no mean task.

The printing of scores and parts and the resulting dissemination of music contributed to the standardisation of the orchestra by demanding a settled constitution of at any rate the basic elements of the orchestra. Haydn had unparalleled opportunities of experimenting with orchestral effects and he availed himself of them with enthusiasm and success. Mozart was able to benefit from Haydn's work and in their hands the art of orchestration not only budded but burst into magnificent flower both in the concert room and the theatre.

The quadruple division of the orchestra into woodwind, brass, percussion and strings which had always existed in one form or another, now became crystallized into a form which has remained basic until the present day. The string group, complete in itself, flexible, expressive, brilliant and active by nature, provided obvious foundation of tone upon which the orchestral structure was built. The woodwind section consisted of one or two flutes, two oboes and two bassoons. To this ensemble a pair of clarinets became added a little later. Two horns, two trumpets and timpani completed what is usually called the " Classical " orchestra. In the theatre a trio of trombones (alto, tenor and bass) were added with perhaps another pair of horns and some extra percussion such as bass drum, cymbals and triangle, known then as " Turkish music ". Beethoven was the first of the great composers to use all these extra instruments, together with piccolo and double bassoon, in symphonic music. In the finale of the C Minor Symphony three trombones blaze out suddenly with terrific effect, and piccolo and double bassoon add increased height and depth to the orchestra. Beethoven also used two trombones and a piccolo in the Storm movement of the *Pastoral Symphony* (No. 6 in F) and kept the trombones in for the finale as well. In the Ninth Symphony (Choral) he demanded not only three trombones, piccolo and double bassoon but an extra pair of horns and " Turkish music " too. An earlier symphony in which " Turkish music " is used is Haydn's famous *Military* Symphony.

In the early classical period the woodwind suffered from mechanical difficulties and deficiences owing to the lack of a really efficient system of key-work. Their intonation seems to have been not infrequently faulty because there were then no precision tools to produce accurate boring. But Mozart's Concertos for wind instruments show us that there were some fine players in his day and one must suppose that there were also very good instruments to be had by those prepared to insist on good workmanship.

We shall see later when discussing the technique of the horn and trumpet how limited was the scope of these instruments before the invention and perfection of the valves. Yet brilliantly effective use was made of them and their very shortcomings could be a challenge to an inventive and resourceful composer. The timpani, almost always only two in number, were tuned to the tonic and dominant of the piece and the part was written on the notes C and G, the tuning being indicated at the beginning of the movement; C, of course indicated the tonic and G the dominant. The timpani therefore shared with clarinet, horn and trumpet the distinction of being a transposing instrument in early classical days, but it soon came to have its part written as it is today at the sounded pitch.

During the nineteenth century orchestration developed with

great rapidity. Improvements in the manufacture of instruments kept pace with the ever-growing demands of composers and the technical skill and musicianship of orchestral musicians progressed by leaps and bounds.

Beethoven, as well as increasing the size of the orchestra for symphonic music made unprecedented demands on instruments hitherto considered less important. The status of the violas, for instance, was raised by him to one of independence. In his early orchestral works he follows the Mozartian model in making them chiefly double the bass part, but from the *Eroica* onwards they are emancipated and given a much more important part to play in the ensemble. In the Ninth Symphony he trusts the viola section well enough to write for it *divisi* with woodwind and cellos. He also used the horns for solo work and not only for filling in the harmony. We need not go further again than the symphonies for examples—the three-horn passage in the trio of the Scherzo of the *Eroica*, or that for two horns in the corresponding movement of No. 8, and the elaborate solo for the fourth horn in the slow movement of No. 9 at once spring to mind. The timpani too were used by Beethoven in quite new ways, e.g. in Symphony No. 4, first movement, in the passage leading to the recapitulation and in Nos. 8 and 9 where he tunes them to F an octave apart and gives them " solo " parts.

Weber, one of Beethoven's most distinguished contemporaries, used the orchestra in original ways to produce in his operas dramatic and imaginative effects. The opening of the *Oberon* overture is magical in its suggestions of fairy landscapes, and the orchestration of *Der Freischütz* is full of original and felicitous touches. He was one of the first to use the orchestra in such a way as to create atmosphere by the subtle manipulation of tone-colour.

Mendelssohn was also outstanding in orchestral invention. His music for *A Midsummer Night's Dream* is full of grace and delicacy but is by no means an isolated phenomenon among his musical output. Such works as the *Italian* and *Scottish* Symphonies and the *Hebrides* Overture provide further examples of the clarity and beauty of texture which are characteristic of all his work.

Rossini at this time was handling large orchestras in his operas with the greatest possible verve, originality and relish. He did much to pave the way for Meyerbeer, Berlioz and Wagner and the lesser, though charming French operatic composers such as Auber and Boïeldieu.

Before the middle of the century had been reached the problem of making brass instruments, apart from the trombone, capable of playing all the notes of the chromatic scale had been solved, and this not only enabled the brass section to be used alone as a satisfactory unit in passages not only of a fanfare-like character, but provided a means of affording a rich background to strings and woodwind. Fortunately Wagner was at hand to benefit by this, and his enterprise and inventive genius were able to make full use of the new possibilities which it opened up. Sax had invented two new families of instruments, Saxhorns and Saxophones. Of these the Tuba, bass of the Saxhorn family, became a regular member of large orchestras, replacing, as a powerful bass instrument, the unsatisfactory serpent and ophicleide. Saxophones were used by French composers to some extent, but have never become regular orchestral instruments. They do not blend sufficiently well with others, though the E flat alto saxophone in particular has been found to be a satisfactory solo instrument in the orchestra. They have of course found their true niche in the modern dance band, in which they are often cleverly blended with muted trumpets and/or trombones. They are also used in Military bands in many countries. In France they actually form the basis of the Military band and are the " Strings " of that combination just as the Clarinets are in ours. The Saxhorn family is firmly established in the British Brass Band, flugelhorn, tenor horns, baritones, euphonium and bombardons being all members of it.

For a time composers wrote for both natural and valve-horns (waldhörner and ventilhörner) so that we find in scores of the date of *Tannhäuser* one pair of natural and one pair of valve-horns. The cornet-à-pistons was invented also at this time and was used to supplement the natural trumpets in some scores. It has, however, found its proper place in Brass and Military bands; the valve-trumpet is a more suitable instrument for symphony and opera.

Wagner and Berlioz were the two greatest and most original

B

orchestrators of the mid-nineteenth century. Both found that their ideas could only be fully expressed by the use of a very large orchestra. It is amazing to realise that Berlioz' *Sinfonie Fantastique* was begun during the lifetime of Beethoven. Its whole conception seems to belong to a later age, though neither Berlioz nor Wagner would have been the composers they were without the doors which had been opened by the dramatic and stormy genius of Beethoven.

Wagner's was, indeed, one of the most original and dynamically creative minds in any line to appear during the wonderful nineteenth century, which was so prodigal and prolific of discoveries and inventions in the arts and sciences. Berlioz was just as original, perhaps more so since he did not have a Liszt to inspire and egg him on, but he did not possess quite the magnificent span of Wagner's thought and his melodic invention varied very much in distinction and quality. Both men conceived their music from the beginning in orchestral terms and were undaunted by the fact that their demands seemed unpractical at the time.

Both were intensely dynamic personalities whose genius best expressed itself in the theatre and both had an uncanny and unerring imagination and insight into the possibilities of hitherto unexploited instrumental sounds and combinations. Berlioz' *Traité d'Instrumentation* gives an insight into his technical methods and also reveals his magnificently opulent aspirations in the matter of orchestras of gargantuan size. Meanwhile, in Russia, Glinka and Balakirev had laid the foundation of the National School of Composers of which Moussorgsky, Borodin and Rimsky-Korsakov are the brightest ornaments. Of these three Rimsky-Korsakov was by far the most professionally expert and developed his extraordinary natural flair for brilliant orchestral writing in a series of highly coloured works for both stage and concert-platform. He also edited and completed the orchestration of the works of many of his contemporaries, some of whom were only spare-time musicians. He went rather too far in his emendations of the score of Moussorgsky's *Boris*. Moussorgsky was the most original of all this group of composers and his harmonies were not always academically " correct " according to Rimsky-Korsakov who had, rather diffidently, become a professor of harmony and counterpoint somewhat late in his career and was therefore unduly sensitive about " forbidden " consecutives and so on, but his help in the matter of orchestration to Borodin, Liadov and others was invaluable. His book *Principes d'Orchestration* is extremely helpful to students, especially the second volume, which consists of quotations in full score taken from his own works.

Rimsky-Korsakov's scoring is extremely clear and well balanced. It always sounds fresh and new-minted and is admirably fitted to the fanciful, fairy-tale subjects which were so dear to his heart and which evoked from him such captivating musical ideas. He was, fortunately, an excellent teacher, able to hand on the fruits of his experience to his pupils. Such diverse composers as Glazounov and Stravinsky were both pupils of his. In his early works, particularly *L'oiseau de feu*, Stravinsky clearly shows his indebtedness to his master.

Tchaikovsky's style was on the whole more cosmopolitan than that of the nationalist school, but his scores are just as brilliant, well balanced and imaginative as theirs. His last symphony, No. 6 in B. minor *(Pathétique)* is full of originality in the handling of the instruments from first to last. In it the orchestration bears a very large part in conveying the varied moods of the work and is equally successful in expressing gaiety and gloom. His scores are models for the student who may be finding difficulty in achieving clarity, but it must always be remembered that with all the great orchestral composers the musical ideas were conceived orchestrally, and there is a strong possibility that the lack of clarity alluded to may be inherent in the music itself. A thick turgid texture overloaded with contrapuntal lines that have not room to breathe may well be to blame.

Brahms's orchestration has often been described in uncomplimentary terms as dull, turgid, uniformly dark brown in colour and so on. Some passages in his works are awkward to play and difficult for a conductor to balance properly but on the whole, though obviously he often had difficulties in finding the right orchestral lay-out for his music, he did usually succeed in making it sound as he wanted. He viewed with suspicion effectiveness and facility, which can, but need not necessarily, indicate a shallow slickness. His music was to him not something independent of mere scoring—-it could not be that—but it needed much thought to find a presentation which would not distract the mind of the listener from the earnestness of the music.

Richard Strauss's tone-poems, which were direct descendants of those of Liszt, brought into the concert hall the large and colourful Wagnerian orchestra, and he and others, notably Bruckner, enlarged this still more. Quadruple woodwind, four or five trumpets, eight horns and sometimes " Wagner Tubas " were introduced into the huge orchestras demanded by *fin-de-siècle* composers. These formidable combinations of anything up to one hundred players or more proved to be tremendously expensive and are more so today when musicians are paid more fitting fees than used to be customary, and the impoverishment brought about by the first world war made composers think twice about employing " extras ". There can be no doubt, all the same, that grandiose conceptions need imposing forces for their proper realisation and the works of such composers as Strauss, Mahler and Bruckner would have been much reduced in stature if they had been inhibited by financial considerations. What is really extravagant is seen when composers write for a very large number of instruments and never use them all together but only in small contrasted groups. This must surely put a strain on the goodwill of admirers who could otherwise be ready and willing to perform these works.

The lives of some of the composers I have mentioned extended into the twentieth century and others born in the nineteenth and working over the turn of the century have to be regarded as twentieth-century composers.

Of these Debussy and Ravel in France, Sibelius in Finland, Strauss and Mahler in Austria and Elgar in England are some of the most outstanding.

Debussy's contribution to the art of orchestration was unique. The new figures and harmonies which he created needed their own shimmering coats of many colours though they did not necessarily have to have a large orchestra to achieve this end. *L'après-midi d'un faune*, for instance, is very modest in its orchestral demands and yet is quite unlike anything that preceded it and is richly and subtly dressed in orchestral tone. When Debussy did use an orchestra of Wagnerian proportions he used it in a thoroughly un-Wagnerian way, with the greatest economy and fastidiousness. The score of *Pelléas et Mélisande,* for instance, is always transparent, although it glows with many-tinted hues.

Ravel was an exquisite craftsman who delighted in subtle orchestral detail. He took infinite pains over every bar and the result, far from betraying any effort, always sounds spontaneous and right and sparkles like jewels. He was so fond of the orchestra that he orchestrated much of his own piano music without, be it noted, altering the lay-out of the original version.

Sibelius's style was very different. His ideas were mostly strong and direct though he could be tender and lyrical and even " atmospheric " when he wished to be. His music was firmly based on a diatonic melodic idiom but it was unmistakably his own and his orchestration also was highly personal. Each department of the orchestra appeared to be strongly differentiated from the others in his mind, and even in *tutti* passages there was little doubling between them, each section contributing something characteristic to the ensemble. His use of the brass and drums was notably effective and he produced splendid horn effects.

Strauss and Mahler, different though they were temperamentally, both ultimately derive from Wagner. Strauss's music is warmly romantic and can be somewhat sensational too (or so at any rate much of it seemed when it first came out). He needed a large orchestra to give full expression to his ideas. There is much doubling for the sake of richness of texture but there is no thickness or turgidity in his scores and every note is in its right place as befits a composer who admired Mozart beyond all others.

Mahler spent much of his time and energy as a conductor and it is surprising that he found opportunities for writing so many large-scale works. A very emotional, sometimes almost tortured temperament drove him on and this, combined with overwork and indifferent health, resulted in music of a highly intense and individual character. His conducting experience gave him a very intimate knowledge of orchestral effect and it says much for the strength of his individuality that, unlike so many composers who are also executants and spend much time and thought over other men's work, his own music never become merely eclectic or derivative. Wagner and Bruckner exerted the strongest and most enduring influences on him, but he was never anything but himself in his mature works. Elgar's scoring was also highly individual. He too was much influenced by Wagner and Strauss. *The Dream of Gerontius,* though it could never have been written by anyone else, owed much to *Parsifal,* and *Falstaff* ultimately derived from Strauss. The *Enigma* Variations were freer from these influences than his later works and though the scoring is rich there are not nearly so much doubling and opulent mixtures of orchestral tone as are to be found in the symphonies and oratorios. His scores are marked with meticulous attention to details of bowing, phrasing and dynamics. Everything is splendidly balanced and the rich poetry of his music is perfectly matched by its orchestral presentation.

And so we come to the time when the twentieth century had really got under way, and which has been marked by tremendous creative activity. Since 1910, when his first challenging and exciting ballet scores began to appear. Stravinsky has maintained a position of pre-eminence in spite, or perhaps because, of the pliancy of his style. He showed early in his career that he could handle with confidence and originality the largest orchestras, but he also showed himself to be master of smaller ensembles and his careful choice of instruments for any given work bears witness to his use of tone-colour as an integral part of his musical ideas. He started as a Russian Nationalist, and has passed through many idioms and forms of musical speech from neoclassical to serial, yet his music is unmistakably personal whether its thematic content derives from Russian folk-song, Mozart, Grieg, Tchaikovsky or Webern. This uniformity of musical personality in spite of surface changes is due very largely to his mastery of varied rhythms and to his style of instrumentation. This is an exact antithesis of the Elgarian method which Stravinsky has dismissed as organistic. Stravinsky has always been very conscious of the characteristic tone and individuality of each instrument and never cared much for mixtures of tone-colour. This may partly account for the attraction which the music of Schönberg, Webern and Berg at last exerted upon him, overcoming the disapproval he once expressed for their methods. For these composers the orchestra presented a palette of an in-

finite variety of colours which could be put together not as
unison blendings, but polyphonically, in contrast rather than
agreement. They preferred physical combinations of tone to
chemical.

It would be unnecessary and superfluous to continue the
catalogue of composers who have contributed to the corpus of
orchestral music during the present century. Their names would
include many British composers, for it was at the turn of the century that our own music began to assume a character of its own
and to free itself from too much dependence on foreign models.
Among these Holst and Delius might be mentioned as showing
two opposite poles, the one realistic, linear and austere, the other
romantic, harmonic and sensuous. Each used the orchestra in
his own masterly way and adapted his orchestral technique
accordingly. Walton's orchestration is powerful and extremely
expert and professional. In his slow movements he always shows
a fine feeling for subtle shades of orchestral colour, and in the
quick ones his vigorous rhythms and astringent harmonies are
backed up by very characteristic use of the instruments. Both his
musical ideas and his scoring, though highly personal, are
derived from Elgar rather than the British Nationalists. Vaughan
Williams was never very confident of his powers as an
orchestrator, and sought advice from others but he often achieved
very beautiful effects, especially from divided strings. The lay-
out of the *tutti* always bothered him and he always tended to
thicken his textures and upset the balance, but such was the
power of his ideas at their best and his sincerity and artistic con-
viction that one came to feel that a little technical clumsiness
was expected of him and was in fact an intrinsic part of his
make-up. At any rate, he was never in danger of following the
easy path of slickness. The most resourceful and inventive of our
native composers born in the twentieth century is Benjamin
Britten. His greatest successes have been in the fields of opera and
of word-setting in general rather than in purely instrumental
composition. His use of a large orchestra in *Peter Grimes* shows
him to be a master who combines great originality of idea with
unerring technical aptitude. In the many operas he has written
for the limited resources of the English Opera Group he has ex-
tracted from a dozen orchestral musicians extraordinarily varied

effects. This is partly due to his use of alternative instruments (e.g. piccolo and bass flute, cor anglais, bass clarinet played respectively by the flautist, oboist and clarinettist as well as their normal instruments), but still more by his imaginative and often unusual spacing of his instruments, not for the sake of producing a perversely sophisticated effect, but because that and no other is exactly the sound he wants to make in order to fulfil the dramatic need of the moment.

Gramophone and radio have added enormously to the dissemination of musical knowledge during the period which has elapsed since the twenties. Inexpensive pocket scores of works of all styles and periods exist in large numbers. There is no excuse for anyone who is interested in such things to remain ignorant of the sounds of the instruments or of some of the more usual methods which composers use in combining them. There is indeed a danger that a large section of the musical public may become so accustomed to mechanically reproduced music that they do not trouble to attend concerts and so come to forget, or perhaps never realise, how much more satisfying the real thing is and what a big part being a member of an audience at a live performance can play in musical enjoyment. As an aid to study, a supplement to concert and opera-going, and, for those who live far away from centres of music-making, a far-better-than-nothing substitute, the gramophone and radio are admirable, but they should never come to be thought all-sufficient. At the same time too lofty an attitude to broadcasting may stand in the way of hearing a good deal of rarely played music, both old and new.

As an offset to too much reliance on musical mechanisation it is a pleasing sign of the times that many boys and girls of school age are learning orchestral instruments. The formation of National and Regional Youth Orchestras provides something really exciting for young enthusiasts to strive for—membership is keenly sought and highly valued—but for those who do not qualify for these exclusive bodies the school orchestra supplies experience which will be valuable to them all their lives and will teach them more about " musical appreciation " than dozens of lectures could ever do. The learning of a wind instrument is far quicker and less painful than struggling with a violin or cello, and though one hopes that string playing will always continue to be encouraged in schools there seems to be more realisation now than ever before of how much enjoyment can be got from making music together, so that the standard of wind playing and the variety of instruments studied, in spite of ever-looming examinations, is going up steadily and school orchestras need no longer be the ill-assorted and unbalanced collections of instruments they once were.

The above very incomplete outline of the history of orchestration during the last two centuries is intended to show how the orchestra has been used, modified and enlarged by composers in succeeding generations until it has become the wonderful organisation it is today. In spite of the changes that have taken place in it and the improvements in the manufacture of instruments all the components of the classical orchestra are still present in the modern orchestra, and the additional instruments are all adaptations and variants of the original standard instruments. Thus the piccolo and bass flute, the cor anglais and heckelphone, the E flat and bass clarinets and the double bassoon are all extensions upwards or downwards of the normal or parent members of those families. The bass tuba (and the tenor if used) we have seen to be an addition *sui generis,* also the saxophones on the rare occasions when they are used. Some percussion instruments, e.g. wind machine, rattle, whip etc., are comparative newcomers and their numbers can be constantly added to for special effects.

All this talk of large orchestras and unlimited resources must not be allowed to go to the head of the young composer with ambitions to storm the heights with symphonic works. In all departments of art economy of means is both a virtue and a matter of commonsense. This is specially applicable to orchestration, when extras mean a further drain on financially hard-pressed orchestral organisations and concert promoters. Before ordering music paper of thirty staves or more let the composer consider how much he can do without, and whether he works under limitations of his own choosing or those imposed from without, let him look on them as a challenge to his ingenuity and inventive powers. Let him remember that Mozart's great G Minor Symphony was written for what would now be called a chamber orchestra and let him admire the skill of Britten's handling of his little orchestra in *The Turn of the Screw*.

It has often been said that it is easier to write for a large orchestra than a small one. This is not really true because with large orchestras intricate problems of design and balance may present very difficult problems, but it is true that with only a small collection of instruments the composer is faced with a different kind of problem, that of providing contrast and incident and avoiding monotony of colour and thinness of texture. Ideally neither large nor small orchestras should present difficulties. The scoring should be inherent in the composer's original conception. But most composers would agree that things do not always go as smoothly as that.

The student should possess as comprehensive a library of pocket scores as his means will allow, and should keep adding to it. In order to get the most benefit from his scores he needs to cultivate the ability to concentrate on detail, not being content just to glance at a score superficially or only to look at it when he is going to listen to or attend a performance of a work. In the early stages he will find difficulties in dealing with certain instruments and in grasping their normal functions in the orchestra. In that case it is a good plan to listen on the radio or gramophone or at a concert to a work with the score, following with eye and ear the clarinet or horn parts or whatever it is that is giving him trouble. His ear will take in the general sound of the music while his eye will pick out the contribution which his chosen instruments are making to it. It is difficult to take in all the details of a score at once at playing speed and it is a good plan to study a score both before and after listening to a performance instead of hectically trying to follow it while it is being played and then imagining that one knows it. The study of the composer's technical methods by reading the score before and after listening has also the advantage of not interfering with the emotional enjoyment of the music. The more the work has been enjoyed and appreciated the stronger will be the desire to find out afterwards, in a relaxed state of mind, how the composer put it together.

The physical sensation of hearing music is far more vivid than any imaginary sounds conjured up by the mental ear can possibly be, however expert the reader. There is no real emotional thrill to be got from this platonic process and the student should never allow cold blooded analysis to blunt the edge of his musical sensibility and receptiveness.

Here is a suggested list of scores which might form the basis of the students' collection :

HAYDN : Any of the later symphonies, particularly those written for Salomon on the occasion of the composer's second visit to London in 1794.

MOZART : The three great symphonies written in the year 1788 in the space of three months in th keys of E flat (K.543), G minor (K.550), and C major (*Jupiter*, K.551).
Overtures : *Die Zauberflöte, Don Giovanni.*

BEETHOVEN : The nine symphonies. If funds will not allow of purchase of all at one go, the following order is recommended : Nos. 3, 5, 7, 9, 1, 2, 4, 6, 8.
Overtures : *Coriolanus, Leonora* No. 3.

MENDELSSOHN : Italian and Scottish symphonies, Overture and incidental music to *A Midsummer Night's Dream.*
Overture : *Fingal's Cave.*

BERLIOZ : *Sinfonie Fantastique.*
Overture : *Benvenuto Cellini.*

SCHUBERT : *Unfinished* Symphony in B Minor.
C Major Symphony No. 9.
Overture and Ballet Music, *Rosamunde.*

WAGNER : Preludes : *Lohengrin, Tristan und Isolde.*
Overtures : *Tannhäuser, Meistersinger, Parsifal.*
Siegfried Idyll.

RIMSKY-KORSAKOV : *Schéhérazade, Antar.*

LIADOV : Eight Russian Folk songs.

R. STRAUSS : *Till Eulenspiegel, Don Juan.*

TCHAIKOVSKY : Symphonies Nos. 4, 5 and 6. Suite *Casse-Noisette.*
Overture—Fantasy : *Romeo and Juliet.*

DEBUSSY : *Prélude, L'apres-midi d'un faune, La Mer, 3 Nocturnes.*

RAVEL : *Daphnis et Chloe, Ma Mère l'Oye.*

ELGAR : *Enigma* Variations, Introduction and Allegro for Strings, Symphony No. 1, in A flat, Symphony No. 2, in

E flat, Cello concerto, Violin concerto, Suites No. 1 and 2, *The Wand of Youth, Falstaff.*

DELIUS : *Paris, On hearing the first cuckoo in Spring.*

STRAVINSKY : *L'oiseau de feu, Petrouchka, Le Sacre du Printemps, Sinfonie des Psaumes, Agon,* etc.

SCHONBERG : *Variations for Orchestra.* Violin concerto.

WEBERN : 6 *Orchestral pieces.*

BERG : Violin concerto.

VAUGHAN WILLIAMS : Any of the symphonies, particularly the *Pastoral,* Symphony No. 4 in F minor, Symphony No. 6. *Tallis* Fantasia for Strings.

HOLST : Suite *The Planets,* Ballet music from *The Perfect Fool.*

BAX : *The Garden of Fand, Tintagel.*

BARTOK : *Concerto for Orchestra.*

WALTON : Viola Concerto, Symphony No. 1.

BLISS : *Music for Strings.*

BRITTEN : *Variations and Fugue on an air of Purcell. Variations for Strings on a theme of Frank Bridge.*

It must be emphasised that the above are only suggestions. Personal taste of course plays its part in the selection of scores, but we are thinking here of the different methods of orchestration shown by the composers and works concerned rather than of any personal predilections in favour of the music itself though all are works of proved excellence by acknowledged masters. It is of course useless to possess a library of scores unless they can be read with some ease and fluency; I do not mean at the pianoforte so much as in an armchair. To read a score at the pianoforte at anything like playing speed (unless it is a very simple classical slow movement) requires a quickness of eye and hand which only few possess, but aural imagination can be developed by any normally musical person who has the necessary ability to concentrate. The old tag about seeing with the ear and hearing with the eye is as valid as ever, especially when it comes to reading a full score in which familiarity with orchestral sounds has to go hand in hand with fluency in transposition and the reading of the less familiar clefs.

In a later chapter the transposition of certain instruments will be explained and historical and musical reasons given for this apparently anomalous procedure.

With regard to the alto and tenor clefs it is much better to face the slight effort of learning to read them as clefs in their own right than by tricks based on transposing from the treble and bass clefs.

The alto clef is used exclusively for the viola and for no other instrument. Its middle line, middle C, lies exactly midway between the treble and bass staff. Here is middle C written in five different clefs:

G ("treble" or   F ("bass" clef)   C ("alto" clef)
   violin clef)   Used by viola
                                                  only. Also used
                                                  by alto voice in
                                                  old scores.

        C ("tenor" clef)   Not used for
        Used for high   any instrument.
        registers of cello,   Used for soprano
        d o u b l e bass   voice in old
        (rarely), bassoon   scores.
        and tenor trom-
        bone. Also used
        by tenor voice
        in old scores.

Another method of writing high cello parts persisted into comparatively recent times. It is exactly like the notation usually employed for the tenor voice in vocal scores in which the part is written in the treble clef but sounds an octave lower. When the treble clef is used nowadays, as it is for unusually high cello parts, the written pitch is always intended. If there is any doubt about which notation is meant the context should clearly decide especially at the points where changes of clef occur, e.g.

which would now be written :

The whole passage would in actual fact be more likely to be written in the tenor clef, as quick dodgings about from one clef to another are to be avoided in the interests of ease of sight-reading for the players. The old-style use of the bass clef in horn parts will be referred to later when the transposing instruments come to be dealt with.

CHAPTER II

THE STRING AND WOODWIND SECTIONS SEPARATELY CONSIDERED

WE HAVE seen that the orchestra falls into four main divisions or sections, consisting of Strings, Woodwind, Brass and Percussion.

Of these the String section with its homogeneous tone-colour, flexibility, wide range of pitch and dynamics and great expressive power supplies the basic (or diapason) tone throughout the orchestral gamut.

The ear does not tire of String tone as it does of the somewhat less refined sound of wind instruments and extended passages for Strings alone are therefore more frequently met with than those for Wind alone in orchestral works.

The normal arrangement is to divide the violins into two almost equal parts, with usually one or two more in the firsts than the seconds because the first violins naturally have the lion's share of the principal melodic line. Below these, bridging the gap between the violins and cellos, come the violas, usually considerably less in number than either of the violin groups. The cellos are usually about the same in numerical strength as the violas, and the basses a little less. Thus in a normally large symphony orchestra we might find the numbers of players in the five groups of the String section to be 16, 14, 10, 10, 8, and in smaller orchestras the players would be roughly in the same proportion, though there is a tendency to be content with disproportionately few double basses, thereby losing sonority and weakening the foundation.

In small amateur or semi-amateur string orchestras, and of course in similar orchestras of mixed strings and wind, there is

31

often a dearth of violas. If the violists that are available are good, confident players there is no need to be unduly apprehensive on the score of balance. I well remember hearing an eighteenth century string concerto played by a band of fifteen arranged thus: 6, 4, 2, 2, 1, and though in this particular work the violas were divided into firsts and seconds, giving only one viola per part, the result was quite satisfactory. On the other side of the scale I remember a string band of the same size divided thus: 4, 4, 4, 2, 1, which sounded excellent too, with a fine, big sonority for so few players. In such small orchestras of strings uniformity of intonation and bold and confident attack by each individual member are essential to success. Given those qualities in his small force a conductor should be able to get any effect he wants within the dynamic range attainable. It should be self-evident that a small consort of competent performers is far more greatly to be prized than a large number which includes even a few passengers in its ranks. Richter said " I have twelve violins; eleven are good, one is bad; I have twelve bad violins."

All departments of the string section may be subdivided and frequently are in scores written with large forces in view. Elgar's Introduction and Allegro for Strings is laid out for *divisi* first and second violins, violas and cellos practically throughout, as well as a string quartet of soloists, while Vaughan Williams's Fantasia on a theme of Thomas Tallis is written for Double String Orchestra as is Michael Tippett's Concerto for Strings. It is in fact impossible to imagine a work written by a contemporary or near contemporary composer for string orchestra or indeed for full orchestra that does not have recourse to subdivision of the string departments, not infrequently into more than two parts. The leader of each group may also be called upon for solo passages.

The study of scores in which composers have really let themselves go with no expense spared, so to speak, is highly stimulating but in real life the composer and/or orchestrator often finds himself challenged by limited resources. And limited resources should be regarded as a challenge to his ingenuity and resourcefulness. Amateur orchestral societies, school orchestras and the like are practically never complete and are usually curiously balanced (on paper at least). It is well for the beginner to cultivate the habit of cutting his instrumental demands to the minimum even if he is not writing for some specific incomplete orchestra. He will then save himself from a shock when he is asked to supply music for some heterogeneous collection of instruments which is all that happens to be available at the time. I shall deal to the best of my ability with some of the problems that may arise in such circumstances later in the book.

To continue our preliminary study of the sections of the orchestra we will now turn to the woodwind. This normally consists of a pair each of flutes, oboes, clarinets and bassoons. The second flute may be called upon to interchange with piccolo, the second oboe with cor anglais, the second clarinet with bass clarinet. It is unusual to find a double bassoon unless there are two ordinary bassoons as well. The reason for the second player alternating with the " extra " instrument is self-evident when we realise that the first player is the soloist on his instrument and cannot be spared for other duties, nor should his embouchure be impaired by changing to the other instrument during the course of a piece, though naturally in writing for single instruments and not pairs this consideration goes by the board.

Britten in his small-scale operas which only employ an orchestra of a dozen or so players in all obtains a wide range of colour from his woodwind soloists, the flute alternating not only with piccolo but with alto (sometimes called bass) flute also, and the oboe and clarinet frequently changing to cor anglais and bass clarinet and back again. When writing for some particular amateur or semi-amateur band it would be most unwise to demand such changes without enquiring beforehand whether the players possess the alternative instruments. Professional players may lose many engagements unless they possess the more usual members of their chosen instruments' family. Bassoon players cannot however, be relied upon to possess double bassoons, which are very expensive and cumbersome.

In works written for triple or quadruple woodwind the third or fourth player respectively may play the alternative instrument throughout but if the composer desires it he must be prepared to interchange with the normal instrument.

There is not much point in changing to the alternative instrument for anything but a solo passage or at any rate one in which

G

the special tone-colour and character of that instrument are indispensable. It is a good plan, if the context permits, to give an instrument to which a change has been made a few unobtrusive passages before its important solo entry so as to give the player a chance of warming it up and making any slight adjustments of intonation that may be necessary, but in the case of the cor anglais this would only be possible in a fairly fully scored passage as its tone is decidedly penetrating.

The woodwind section as a whole is by far the weakest. It is easily swamped by the strings and still more by the brass, but if it is used with due knowledge of effect it can add a good deal of brilliance to the ensemble even when strings and brass are exerting their full force. In classical times one of the main functions of the woodwind was to give a simple harmonic background to busy string figuration (Ex. 1). In using woodwind melodically a single instrument might be used, but the flute often doubled in the higher octave a melody on the oboe, clarinet, or

violins and sometimes the melody would be given also to the bassoon in the lower octave, presenting a three-octave combination. This was done to give weight and carrying power to the tune as well as making a very pleasant sound. (Ex. 2.)

A three-octave unison on all the eight woodwind instruments is quite powerful. In Ex. 3 the background is provided by strings *pp* against which this incisive phrase stands out in very bold relief. Of course, if a piccolo were added to such an ensemble there would be a gain in brilliance and penetrating power without the addition of another player if the piccolo were played by the second flautist (the piccolo sounds an octave higher than written).

In Ex. 4 we find a three-octave unison of double woodwind holding its own against quite powerful forces. The pairs of oboes and clarinets are each playing in octaves. Note the three different dynamic markings, *mf*, *f* and *ff* which it is very important to observe in order to achieve a satisfactory balance and perspective of tone. The piccolo is written in actual unison with the flutes. If

it had been placed an octave higher the effect would have been too shrill and piercing here. Very high notes on the piccolo in *forte* and *fortissimo* should be looked upon as a resource only available in fully scored passages. The piccolo need not, however, be thought of as an instrument only suitable for loud passages. It can have a most charming effect in *piano* and *pianissimo* doubling a lightly accompanied violin or flute melody at the octave above.

Clarinets and bassoons make excellent four-part harmony especially if the music is ecclesiastical in style and a quiet, tranquil feeling is wanted. Ex. 5 shows these instruments used in this way in the natural order of pitch (except for the first chord). In Ex. 6 the parts are dovetailed, the second clarinet playing below the first bassoon :

This method of dovetailing is often used in laying out chords for wind, especially between oboes and clarinets, in order to obtain a good mixture of tone between instruments of different timbre. But it should not be used mechanically and without regard to pitch. The low notes of the flute are relatively weak, and it would be a great mistake to write the first oboe above the second flute unless the pitch were pretty high. The low notes of the oboe are, however, powerful and rather coarse and if dovetailing brought the second oboe below, say, D above middle C it would be better to score the chord in the natural order of pitch of the instruments. The high notes of the bassoon are thin in tone and this, again, will influence the choice between dovetailing and the natural order.

A few examples will explain this more clearly than words:

(d)   Clarinets in B flat

Chord (a) would have a bright uniform sound. Dovetailing occurs between oboes and clarinets but nowhere else.

In chord (b) the first oboe is placed above the second flute. This does not give the best balance. The dovetailing of clarinets and bassoons results in the first bassoon being placed in its rather thin high register, impairing the tone of the whole chord. Chord (c) would only be satisfactory in *piano* or *pianissimo* but would be quite good at those levels. There is no dovetailing. In chord (d) the oboes would be too prominent especially the second oboe. It is not possible to produce quiet tone at the bottom of the oboe's compass. The flutes would be hopelessly outclassed. The two bassoons together on the low E flat would also be difficult to subdue to a real *piano*. We see here a bad effect due to injudicious dovetailing of flutes and oboes.

Ex. 8 shows two different methods of obtaining a good mixture of oboe and clarinet tone. Note that in both sets of chords the flutes are given the two top notes. In the first set the oboes enclose the clarinets. In the second set the clarinets are treated as higher instruments than the oboes:

Where there is massive brass scoring it is very effective to double the two upper parts at the octave above on flutes, oboes and clarinets as in Ex. 9:

(Brass in full harmony below)

Much brilliance is added to the brass by this means. If woodwind is placed among the brass in unison doubling it does no good and may indeed do harm by spoiling the purity of the brass tone. Tchaikovsky did, however, sometimes double his trumpets at the unison with oboes with the intention, no doubt, of giving the trumpets additional incisiveness.

It is, of course, one of the main functions of the Woodwind section to provide solo instruments of varied and contrasted tone-colour. Flute, Oboe, Clarinet and Bassoon have each of their own characteristics and idiosyncrasies and it is the orchestrator's business to develop a sympathetic appreciation of these and to acquire by listening, by the study of scores and, if possible, by consulting players, some insight into the sort of melodies and phrases which suit each one best both from the technical and aesthetic point of view.

Very good results can be obtained from a five-piece woodwind section consisting of one flute, one oboe, two clarinets and one bassoon. The two clarinets with their great capabilities in the way of blending with the other instruments have a very useful cohesive effect on the woodwind texture. Their wide compass and flexibility and adaptability of tone in the hands of good players make a pair of clarinets a very desirable thing in both small and large orchestras. Passages in thirds and sixths on two clarinets are always delightful to the ear.

CHAPTER III

TRANSPOSING INSTRUMENTS. WOODWIND AND HORNS IN
COMBINATION WITH EACH OTHER AND WITH STRINGS

ANYONE WHO has looked at an orchestral score will realise that
the parts of some instruments are not written at the pitch of the
actual sounds. The instruments concerned are called transposing
instruments. These comprise, in the normal orchestra without
" extras ", the clarinet, horn and trumpet. The double bass is
also a transposing instrument, its part being written an octave
higher than the sounds played.

In order to avoid confusion between written and sounded
notes players of transposing instruments use the expression " concert pitch " to indicate the actual sounds. Thus a clarinet player
who is uncertain of the correctness of a note in his part may ask
if it is " A concert " or " C sharp concert " or whatever it may
be and the same holds good for all players of transposing instruments.

Early clarinets could only be played easily in keys with not
more than one sharp or flat. Three clarinets were then in use,
in C, B flat and A. The C clarinet was non-transposing and was
used for the keys of C, F and G. The B flat instrument which
was built a tone flat and whose part was therefore written a tone
higher to compensate for this could still finger the scales of C, F
and G but they would sound those of B flat, E flat and F. The
clarinet in A was built a minor third flat, its part was written a
minor third higher and its scales of C, F and G gave, in sound,
those of A, D and E. Orchestral music was rarely written in
keys with more than three sharps or flats; for instance the nine
symphonies of Beethoven are in C, D, E flat, B flat, C minor, F,

A, F and D minor. Slow movements were sometimes written in
four flats, as in Beethoven's C minor symphony and Mozart's late
E flat symphony, but composers avoided keys of even that degree
of remoteness for their quick movements as a general rule. The
C clarinet appears to have been inferior in tone to the other two
and when improvements in manufacture had made the fingering easier in keys up to two or even three sharps and flats it was
possible to discard the C instrument altogether. The B flat and A
clarinets have remained in use up to the present day, the B flat
being used for flat keys and the A for sharp keys. This enables
clarinet parts to be written in easy keys whatever the key signature of the piece may be. A few instances will make this clear:

Key signature of piece   Key signature of Clarinet

Orchestral music is still rarely written in remote keys (when it is written in any key at all) so it will be seen that clarinet parts will seldom have even three sharps or flats. If the original key be C major the key of the B flat clarinet part will be D, whilst if it be G the A clarinet will probably be used, playing in B flat. But the A clarinet is quite often used for movements in C major, giving its part a three-flat signature. Similarly the B flat instrument may be used for the key of G, giving its part a three-sharp signature. In these instances the choice will depend on whether the music modulates to or possesses an important section on the flat or sharp side of the original key.

Composers sometimes change clarinets in midstream. In the Siegfried Idyll for instance the main body of the work is in E major but there is an extended section in A flat in which the wind instruments play a very important part. Wagner therefore changes from the A clarinets, which are naturally used in the E major portion, to B flat clarinets for the flat key, and back again to the A instruments when the E major tonality is restored.

If such changes are made in the course of a movement plenty of time should be given for the player to breathe into the unused instrument to warm it up. In the Siegfried Idyll the first clarinet is a little more fortunate than his colleague; the number of bars rest for the two players is 27 and 17 respectively in which to make the change from the A to the B flat instrument, while both have eight bars in which to take up their A clarinets again. The tempo of the music is fairly slow four-in-a-bar. Eight bars of quick two-four time would hardly be sufficient. In *Préludes à l'après midi d'un faune* Debussy expects his clarinets to change with breath-taking speed—only two beats are allowed for the change from A to B flat. A few bars earlier they have nearly four bars rest in which they could do it, transposing the next four bars down to a semitone. (See Fig 4 in the score). The change back to the A instruments (after Fig. 9) is almost as quick, but is not really necessary as no undue difficulties arise if the B flat clarinets are retained and the parts transposed.

Players much prefer not to have to change clarinets for short sections in the course of a movement and often disregard the composer's instruction to do so, preferring to transpose unless this leads to excessively awkward passages. The action and key-work of the modern clarinet make it much easier to play in remote keys than it used to be, in fact there are signs that the A clarinet may in time become obsolete. The B flat instrument is exclusively used in military and dance bands.

The "extra" woodwind instruments are all transposing so that the players of the normal instruments can read and finger the notes just as they are accustomed to do. Thus the piccolo is a transposing instrument to the extent that its part sounds an octave higher than it is written and the bass (or more accurately alto) flute sounds a fourth below the written note and is therefore sometimes called the alto flute in G. The cor anglais is the alto of the oboe family and sounds a fifth below the written note whilst the heckelphone or bass oboe (a rare instrument) sounds an octave below. There is a small clarinet in E flat sounding a minor third above and a bass clarinet in B flat (formerly also in A) sounding a major ninth below. A contrabass clarinet also in B flat exists and is used in American Symphonic Bands (corresponding to our Military Bands, but a good deal larger) which sounds two octaves and a tone below.

The double bassoon (contrafagotto) sounds, like the string bass, an octave below the written note.

The reader will by now have grasped what is meant by an instrument being "in" a key. An instrument is to said to be B flat, A, G, F, E flat and so on if the natural scale of C played on it produces one of those scales. All that is necessary is to remember whether the transposition is up or down and whether an octave has to be added to such transpositions. If the normal pitch-level of an instrument is known, common sense will tell the score-reader whether the transposition is up or down.

It must be added that some scores are printed with all instruments at concert pitch. This applies mainly to contemporary music based on highly chromatic idioms. Serial music in particular is written in this way (with of course no key signature) in order to show more clearly to the eye its structural organisation. Everything is written strictly at the sounded pitch, even the piccolo, double bassoon and double bass, leger-lines appearing in dazzling profusion in their parts.

The horns are so often used in combination with the woodwind and much use has always been made of long held notes to belonging to both the woodwind and brass sections. The classical composers wrote their slow movements mostly for woodwind, two horns and strings, omitting trumpets and drums, though there are exceptions to this procedure.

The cool quiet notes of the horns blend admirably with woodwind and much use has always been made of long held notes to give cohesion and substance to the orchestral texture.

In classical scores horns in all keys are found, particularly in C, D, E flat, E, F, G, A, B flat alto and B flat basso. The reason for this was that the horn was severely limited in the number of notes it could play until the valve-mechanism was invented and perfected so that it could play a complete chromatic scale throughout its compass. The notes playable on the natural horn (i.e. without valves) were those of the harmonic series from a fixed fundamental which was always thought of as C. The fundamental note itself was (and is still) so difficult to coax out that the bottom note for practical purposes was the second harmonic. The player by means of lip pressure which he learned to control with precision was able comfortably to select from the series the required harmonic at least up to the twelfth. What he was really doing was to cause the air column to vibrate fractionally. It is obvious that the longer the column the more easily can it be persuaded to give the higher harmonics. Therefore, horns in C, B flat basso and to a lesser extent those in D and E flat could be used up to the sixteenth harmonic much more readily than the shorter lengths of tubing required for the higher-pitched horns.

In the natural horn the main body of the instrument remains unchanged, crooks of varying length being fitted to it to give the different keys.

The following is the harmonic series based on C:

The seventh harmonic is flat; the intervals between the notes get smaller as the series is ascended, and the minor third between G and B flat is thus a little smaller than that between E and G. The three whole tones formed by the seventh, eighth, ninth and tenth harmonics are likewise not exactly the same, though those between eight and nine and nine and ten are near enough for the latter to be adjusted by lip pressure. The eleventh harmonic is slightly sharp, being nearly midway between F and G. Composers often wrote F sharp, the player " pinching up " to reach this note.

The thirteenth and fourteenth harmonics were not used much, being well-nigh impossible to play in tune, but the fifteenth and sixteenth were available, especially in low-pitched horns.

Other notes were obtainable by the process known as hand-stopping, the right hand being thrust further into the bell of the instrument than its normal position. But these notes were muted and sounded quite different from the open notes.

We can thus see why the horn was a transposing instrument. Its fundamental could be changed by inserting a whole variety of crooks but was always thought of as C. This was much simpler and easier for the player. The C major notation was in principle very much like the sol-fa system which calls the key note Doh whatever its pitch is and works from that on the basis of relative pitch.

The introduction of valves altered the whole technique of writing for the horn, which could now play in any key without having to change crooks. Seven different fundamentals with their attendant series were now instantaneously at the player's command. The valves opened lengths of tubing which lowered the series by a semitone, a tone and a minor third respectively. Combinations of these were able to give a major third, a fourth and a diminished fifth below the open note (represented by C). The seven series, each a semitone apart, yielded a chromatic scale, several notes of which could be produced with different fingering, that is as harmonics in different series. By general agreement the valve-horn in F became the standard instrument, as it has a very useful working compass for orchestral purposes. Its fundamental open note continued, however, to be written as C. It is therefore still a transposing instrument in F, its part being written a fifth above the sounds required.

Whatever key the horn is in, its written part is always higher than the sounded notes. Thus horn in C parts sound an octave lower, those for horns in D sound a minor seventh lower, in E flat a major sixth, in E a minor sixth, in F a fifth, in G a fourth, in A a minor third and in B flat alto a tone. The B flat basso horn is an octave lower than the B flat alto and sounds an octave and a tone lower than the written note.

For the lowest notes of the horn the bass clef is used. There used to be a convention whereby in the bass clef the transposition was reversed and the reader of scores has to be prepared for this. For instance, horns in D would transpose up a tone in the bass clef instead of down a seventh, and horns in F up a fourth instead of down a fifth. This notation is still in use though for a long time many composers have used the more sensible method of writing the same transposition in both clefs. It is customary to keep to the treble clef except for the deepest notes, using leger lines below the staff freely. This is the traditional practice to which horn-players are accustomed and they prefer it to constant changes of clef for short passages just for the sake of avoiding a few leger lines.

Here is a little phrase characteristic of natural horns:

Ex: 12

On the horns in C it would sound

On the horns in D it would sound

On the horns in E♭ it would sound

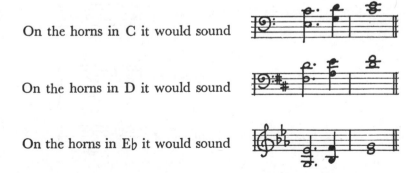

On the horns in E♮ it would sound

On the horns in F it would sound

On the horns in G it would sound

On the horns in A it would sound

On the horns in B♭ alto it would sound

On the horns in B♭ basso it would sound

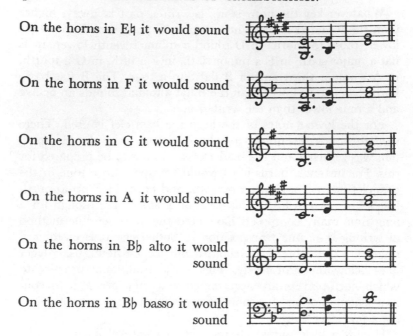

In the old bass clef notation :

Ex: 13

On the horns in C it would sound

On the horns in D it would sound

On the horns in E♭ it would sound

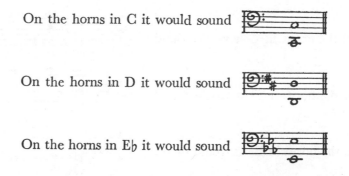

And so on, the transposition being up instead of down except for that of the B♭ basso horns which would of course sound :

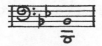

For the score reader the simplicity of natural horn parts compensates for their multiplicity of crooks. They were usually (though not always) pitched in the key of the movement so that C represents the tonic and G the dominant and so on.

Most modern horn players use the " double horn " in F and B flat alto. Their part continues to be written as for F horn, that is a fifth above concert pitch. By manipulating a switch which works instantaneously the player can convert it into a B flat alto instrument. He can by this means attack high notes with greater confidence and precision than he could on the ordinary " single " horn in F. For instance C above middle C instead of being taken as the twelfth harmonic from F could be played as the ninth from B flat and since the harmonics, as we have seen, get closer and closer together as the harmonic series ascends, the lower harmonics must obviously be easier to pick out.

Another advantage arises from the ability to execute a leap from one note to another without much change of embouchure just by the use of the switch.

These are technical matters which only concern the player. The double horn was invented in order to help performers to keep abreast with the demands of composers. The effect on composers and orchestrators is to reduce some of the qualms they may still have when writing high horn parts. It should, all the same, be remembered that hornists cannot be expected to stay up among the high harmonics for long at a time. The lip soon tires and may actually become sore, which means farewell to accuracy and precision in spite of the B flat switch. This mechanical aid has, incidentally, been a great comfort to hornists in playing classical-period horn parts written for high horns in A and B flat alto etc. The *tessitura* of such parts makes their execution on ordinary F horn tiring and therefore precarious especially in strenuous movements like the finale of Beethoven No. 7.

D

We have mentioned that the horns can be effectively used to sustain a note (often in octaves) for several bars. This is useful in binding together a passage which otherwise would be too cut up and disjointed. Here is an example from Beethoven's *Leonora* No. 3 Overture :

The passage continues similarly for another five bars, the horns holding their G to the end. Beethoven uses the same technique in *Coriolanus* where the violins have the second subject tune accompanied by cello arpeggios to which the held horn octaves give a sustaining pedal effect. It must be remembered that the possible length of time that a note can be sustained varies very much with the dynamic force required. About forty seconds would be a fairly comfortable limit at the piano or pianissimo range, whereas only about twelve to fifteen seconds would be possible forte. Long notes high up in the horn's compass are fatiguing at all dynamic levels.

Wagner obtains a good uniform and well-balanced sound at the beginning of the *Tannhäuser* Overture from Clarinets, Horns and Bassoons:

" Ventilhörner " (Valve-horns) are specified in the score. There is another pair of horns, " Waldhörner " (Natural horns) used in this work which was written early in the history of the valve-horn. Note the use of two bassoons in unison to balance the weight of the four instruments above, also the way in which the clarinet and horn tone are blended by interweaving the second clarinet and second horn. All parts are marked *sehr gehalten* (well sustained).

Whilst on the subject of Wagner I would recommend a thorough study of the score of the *Siegfried Idyll*. Among its many perfections it shows to admiration how to use a pair of horns in a small ensemble.

In the normal symphony orchestra four horns are used. These have been employed from time to time as a solo quartet in four-part harmony. Early examples of this are to be found in Weber's *Der Freischütz* and Rossini's *Semiramide* Overtures. The *Valse des Fleurs* from Tchaikovsky's *Casse-Noisette* Suite (opening tune) is a later example and a more modern one is to be found in Benjamin Britten's *Variations and Fugue on a Theme of Purcell* (or *The Young Person's Guide to the Orchestra*) p. 36 of Min. score.

When four horns are used the usual practice is to regard them as two pairs, laying out chords thus:

The third horn being the "leader" of the second pair plays above the second. In the Britten example his procedure is not adopted, no doubt because the two pairs of horns are mainly playing in opposition to one another, each in thirds. The unison of four horns fortissimi is powerful and invigorating. There is a fine example in Strauss's *Don Juan*. Here is a short phrase from Bartok's *Concerto for Orchestra* (p. 79 Min. Score). It is entirely unaccompanied:

The effect of the three trumpets coming in on the horns' last note is tremendous. In the very large orchestras used by Strauss, Mahler and other post-Wagnerian composers eight horns may be found. Mahler's third symphony opens with eight horns playing in unison. Holst's *Planets* Suite contains parts for six horns. The rest of the wind section in such scores is proportionately large.

Although the main function of the horns is to supply richness and nobility of tone to the inner harmonies the horn is often used as a solo instrument and many composers have availed themselves of its expressive or heroic quality and have written fine melodies for it. The obbligato horn part which Bach wrote to accompany the bass solo in the *Quoniam* of the B minor Mass must have been a tough nut for natural horn-players to crack. It gives modern players plenty to think about. Other familiar horn solos which come readily to mind occur:

(1) At the opening of Beethoven's *Fidelio* Overture (allegro).
(2) In the Trio of the same composer's Scherzo in the Eighth Symphony.
(3) In the slow movement (fourth horn part) of the Ninth Symphony. This part was most probably written for an early valve instrument with possibly two pistons instead of three.
(4) In the Nocturne from Mendelssohn's music to *A Midsummer Night's Dream*.
(5) In the Andante Movement of Tchaikovsky's Fifth Symphony.
(6) At the beginning of Delius's *Appalachia*.
(7) At the opening of the slow movement of Vaughan Williams's *Pastoral Symphony*.

not to mention the famous *Till Eulenspiegel* solo and Siegfried's horn-call in *The Ring*. Wagner's use of eight horns at the beginning of *The Rhinegold* must not be forgotten with its highly evocative suggestions of watery depths based endlessly and hypnotically on the chord of E flat.

A word should be said here about the notation of modern horn parts. We have seen that in pre-valve days a horn part was always written in the key C, the crook being indicated. This practice continued after the introduction of the valve horn and the virtual disappearance of the natural horn in spite of the instrument having become fully chromatic. It still seems to be a matter of individual idiosyncrasy whether a composer uses a key-signature or not. Many conductors favour the method of writing without key-signatures because it is a help to have horn (and trumpet) parts clearly differentiated from the other instruments in the score and is thus an aid to score-reading. For this reason and from years of habit I do not myself write key-signatures for horns or trumpets as a general rule. If this method is used it is absolutely vital to be careful to put in all the necessary accidentals if time at rehearsal is not to be wasted.

We have in this chapter given a few indications of the possibilities possessed by the horns as individual soloists or as a pair or quartet in the orchestra, combined with woodwind and strings. We shall give them further consideration as members of the Brass Section in the next chapter.

CHAPTER IV

THE TRUMPET, CORNET, TROMBONES AND TUBA.
THE BRASS SECTION AS A WHOLE

THE HISTORY of trumpet technique closely resembles that of the horn.

The sounds of the natural trumpet were limited to the notes of the harmonic series even more rigidly than those of the natural horn, since hand-stopping was not practicable on the trumpet.

Like the horn the natural trumpet possessed crooks which could put it into any required key and its part was written in the key of C. In the days of Bach and Handel the D trumpet seems to have been the favourite, and D major was therefore predominantly used for movements of a festive or joyful nature. But D was by no means the only possible trumpet key. At that time composers expected their trumpeters to be able to play brilliant passages from the eighth up to the sixteenth harmonic where scalewise movement was possible.

Here is a passage from three trumpets from Bach's *Mass in B minor* :

This passage sounds a tone higher than the written pitch.

If the reader will refer back to Ex. 12 the little phrase there given will sound an octave higher than the pitch at which it is sounded by the horns when crooked in C to F inclusive, thus trumpets in C sound the written note, in D the tone above, in E flat and E natural the minor and major thirds above and in F the fourth above. The trumpet in G was not much used, trumpets in C or D being favoured for movements written in that key. Trumpets in B flat and A transpose in the same way as horns in B flat alto and A, or as Clarinets in B flat and A, a tone and a minor third down respectively.

When valve trumpets were introduced the trumpet in F was used for flat keys and that in E for sharp. Here is a quotation showing the use of a valve trumpet in F from the Prelude to *Parsifal*:

sounding a fourth higher (in A flat major).

And here is one from Sibelius' Symphony No. 1 in E minor for three E trumpets:

sounding a major third higher (in E minor).

In the two middle movements of this symphony, which are in

the keys of E flat and C major respectively, Sibelius writes for trumpets in F. (The horns are similarly used in E in the two outer movements and in F in the inner ones.)

I have mentioned these various transpositions as an aid to reading the scores of works which employ them, but the only trumpet in general use today is that in B flat. Composers often write for trumpets in C which of course entail no problems of transposition, but the parts are played on B flat trumpets and it is therefore best to write for these. Many players possess a trumpet in D for playing high eighteenth-century parts and they also sometimes use it for a part in a modern work whose tessitura lies mainly in the high register.

Both horn and trumpet players are expert at transposition as indeed they have to be. When a part written for a trumpet in E is played on a trumpet in B flat the player has to transpose it an augmented fourth or diminished fifth up, to take an extreme instance.

Some grandeur and nobility of tone seems to have been lost in discarding the trumpets in F and E and substituting that in B flat, but there has been a gain in flexibility and agility of execution. The trumpet in A is not used. The A shank which used to be fitted to the B flat instrument made intonation uncertain unless there was very careful readjustment of the lengths of tubing opened by the valves. The B flat trumpet is therefore used in both flat and sharp keys as a general rule.

The cornet in B flat was used in the orchestra in the latter half of the nineteenth and early twentieth century, not to replace the trumpet but as an addition to the normal brass ensemble. French composers were particularly prone to use a pair of cornets as well as two trumpets, and in this country, Elgar (in *Cockaigne*) and Vaughan Williams (in his *London Symphony*) also scored for cornets as well as trumpets. Another well known example that comes to mind is provided by *Petrouchka*.

The cornet, which is capable of rapid and precise execution, has a less distinguished tone than the trumpet and the style of the average cornet player is apt to leave a good deal to be desired especially when vibrato is indulged in, as it very often is. The establishment of the B flat trumpet as the normal orchestral instrument has rendered the cornet unnecessary in the orchestra since both are practically equally agile. In the Military and Brass band the cornet comes into its own though in large and well equipped Military bands a pair of trumpets is usually to be found and optional parts are provided for trumpets by most composers and arrangers.

Composers when writing for full Symphony Orchestra often use three trumpets. They are thus able to write consecutive triads, six-three and six-four chords and other three-note combinations which are extremely effective on three trumpets. The trumpet is a useful solo instrument if the right type of music is written for it. That this need not necessarily be of a fanfare, ceremonial or martial character has been demonstrated by Britten in his *Midsummer Night's Dream* in which a solo trumpet is associated throughout with Puck and is called upon to play very spirited and brilliant passages.

The trombone works essentially on the same principle as the horn and trumpet, though its actual mechanism is different. The pitch of the fundamental is lowered by pushing out the slide, and seven positions each lowering the pitch by a semitone are used. The notes of the harmonic series up to the eighth harmonic are obtained by lip pressure and embouchure, just as they are on the horn and trumpet, and expert players can reach the twelfth harmonic.

The instrument is thus fully chromatic and always has been, so that there has never been any necessity for transposition of trombone parts. Two tenor trombones (in B flat) and one bass trombone (in G) are the normal constituents of the trombone group. The German bass trombone is in F. The tenor trombone's seven positions are shown here up to the eighth harmonic in each case :

Ex: 21

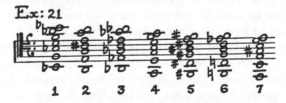

1   2   3   4   5   6   7

The fundamental notes can be produced and are an octave lower than the bottom notes shown above :

Ex: 22

The first three or so of these fundamental notes—they are called " pedal notes "—are easier to coax out of the instrument than the rest, but a skilful player can manage all of them. They are not used much as they have a rather coarse tone which is only suitable for special effects.

The Bass or G trombone is a minor third below the tenor and works in exactly the same way, its fundamentals descending from G by semitones to C sharp.

Formerly an alto trombone in E flat, a fourth above the tenor trombone in pitch, was used, the trio then consisted of alto, tenor and bass trombones. The parts were written respectively in the alto, tenor and bass clefs. The invention of the valve trumpet made the alto trombone redundant and it was found more useful to employ two tenors and a bass. The two tenors are usually written together on one staff of the score in the tenor or bass clefs, but the practice of writing them both in the alto clef was carried on by some composers until quite recent times. Elgar used the alto clef in the *Enigma* Variations and Sibelius in *Tapiola* writes the first trombone part sometimes in the alto clef and sometimes in the bass, according to pitch, while the second and third trombones share between them a bass clef staff. The bass clef has now become the customary clef for the tenor trombone, the tenor clef being used for high passages to save leger lines.

The trombone is an extremely powerful instrument and the trio of trombones gives great weight and sonority to the orchestral *tutti*. It is, however, a mistake to confine the trombones to loud passages. Their pianissimo is extremely effective and can be toned down to a very quiet level of sound. The unison of three trombones is well demonstrated in the very well known passage in the *Tannhäuser* Overture. No undue force is necessary here to bring the melody of the *Pilgrims' Chorus* through the accompanying orchestral texture.

Trombone players have moved a long way since the early days of their entry into the orchestra, and quite a lot of agility is expected of them. But the real character of the trombone is shown when it is used in a manner which shows appreciation of its inherent nobility and dignity. There is something to be said for Mendelssohn's refusal to write for trombones in secular music. Chords for trombones must be spaced with great care. There is a tendency among inexperienced orchestrators to write too low for them. The works of the great orchestral composers must be studied to find out the many ways in which trombones can be most effectively used. The study of scores, by the way, is not recommended in order that the student may learn a repertoire of tricks at second hand, but to act as a stimulus to invention and to inculcate a sensible and practical attitude to the business of writing for instruments.

The remaining brass instrument in general use is the bass tuba. This is of great use in strengthening the bass line and giving 16 ft. tone to the brass section. Its tone is quite different from that of the trombones, though in piano and pianissimo passages this is not so noticeable as it is at higher dynamic levels. It is capable of a considerable degree of execution if wide leaps are avoided and can give a splendid bass staccato, almost a pizzicato effect. Solos are sometimes written for it, e.g. in the Dancing Bear scene in Stravinsky's *Petrouchka* and in *Bydlo* from the *Pictures from an Exhibition* in Ravel's orchestration, though the latter goes rather perilously high and is safer on the euphonium or " tenor tuba " as it is called in the orchestra. There is also a fine pianissimo passage (with string basses) for tuba, low in its compass this time, in Wagner's *Faust* Overture. Most late nineteenth-century and twentieth-century composers have used the tuba. Richard Strauss used tenor and bass tubas as solo instruments (particularly the tenor) in *Don Quixote*. Sibelius shows great appreciation of its special qualities in his symphonic works though rather surprisingly he omits it from the score of the large orchestra he employs in *Tapiola*. Vaughan Williams even wrote a concerto for the bass tuba.

The *Wagner Tubas* which were made specially for *The Ring* to Wagner's specification need not detain us. There are very few in existence. Some other composers have made use of them (e.g.

Bruckner, Strauss and Stravinsky), but they have never really caught on. Wagner used a quartet of these instruments, two sometimes in E flat, sometimes in F, and two in B flat which could be played by the fifth, sixth, seventh and eighth horn players alternately with horns. They are played with ordinary horn mouth-pieces.

THE HORNS USED AS MEMBERS OF THE BRASS SECTION.

We have seen that the horns perform a dual function in the orchestra. They are often used to give colour and warmth to the woodwind and string ensemble, their beautifully round and re-fined tone blending in excellently. But they are, after all, brass instruments and blend admirably with trumpets and trombones. The tuba, incidentally, goes very well below a horn quartet. The power of a horn is about half that of the trumpet or trombone in forte or fortissimo passages and two horns in unison are often used to supply notes which would otherwise be missing from brass chords. Here is a brief example of this from Rimsky-Korsakov's *Snegourochka*. Wind and strings also take part but the brass is complete in itself:

Ex: 23

When devising the lay-out of chords on the brass it is well to make sure that the trumpets and trombones have the essential notes of the chord. Horns can then be added, either filling gaps in the chord or doubling at the unison notes given to trumpets and/or trombones. The beginner is sometimes puzzled about what to give the horns in a *tutti* when the trombones are playing. The thing to do is to distribute to the horn quartet such notes as will lie in a comfortable part of their compass and will not, by over-doubling, upset the balance of the chord. A few examples will show some *faulty arrangements* of brass chords containing horns. All are imagined being played loudly:

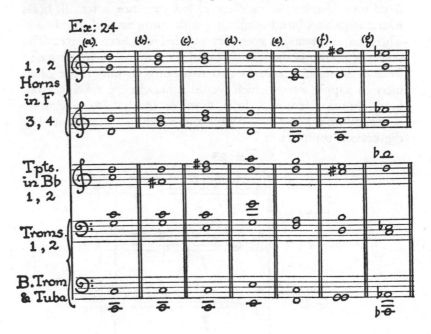

Criticisms:

Chord (a)   Third of chord too weak (only on third horn).
      (b)   Third of chord too strong (on second and third horns and second trumpet).
      (c)   Third of chord again too strong (on second and fourth horns and first trumpet). Second trombone ill placed.

(d) Fifth from root too strong (on all four horns, first trumpet and first and second trombones).

(e) All top and bottom. Too much gap between the trumpets and the rest. All horns but the third are wasted in doubling trombones instead of helping to fill the gap.

(f) Too much third of chord here again (on first horn, first trumpet and first trombone). Poor spacing and distribution of notes.

(g) Only the first trombone has the fifth of the chord. The root and third are far too prominent and general spacing is unsatisfactory.

When only two horns are used, one of them may be wasted if they are both given the same note to play. The balance will be perfectly good if special care is taken with the spacing and lay-out of the trumpet and trombone parts. Dovetailing the horn and trombone parts helps uniformity of tone and balance. Of the following two chords (a) is far preferable to (b)

All these considerations apply equally whether the chords are sustained or detached.

Three trumpets are so often used by composers of today that this number can be regarded as practically normal in the full symphony orchestra. The three trumpets present a perfect balance with the three trombones and triads in close position sound exceedingly brilliant when placed high, e.g.

Contrapuntal writing for brass is very effective. An example of quick contrapuntal writing for trumpets and trombones is to be found in Bartok's Concerto for Orchestra (First Movement, beginning at bar 316). Gabrieli's *Sonata pian e forte* shows how grand slow sixteenth-century counterpoint sounds on modern brass instruments.

Muted Brass:
Mutes are freely used on all brass instruments and produce different tone-qualities according to their softness and hardness and the materials from which they are made (fibre, metal, etc.). They fit into the bells of the instrument and muffle the natural open sounds.

Horn players still use hand stopping by pushing the right hand into the bell if there is no time to insert a mute. The effect is very much the same as that produced by a mute and instantaneous contrasts of open and muted sounds can be obtained in this way. Hand stopping is indicated by a cross over the note.

Muted brass is used at all dynamic levels. The mutes produce a distant, dreamy effect in pianissimo and a fierce, almost savage noise in fortissimo. In *Don Quixote* Strauss obtains a marvellously realistic piece of tone-painting by using rapidly tongued notes on muted brass to represent a herd of sheep. At one time composers were inclined to overdo muted effects and early twentieth-century music abounds in them. The novelty has long worn off and muted brass is only used now as a special and carefully calculated means of expression. The menacing and sinister are well invoked by muted trombones and trumpets in their medium and low registers, not too soft and not too loud, but unless the harmony has distinction the result is likely to sound somewhat meretricious. Muted trumpets can be pert and comic. The second movement Bartok's Concerto for Orchestra contains extended duets for two muted trumpets playing in major seconds—an amusing conceit which of course can never be repeated. Trumpets and trombones using a soft mute and blown softly blend very well with woodwind, especially double reed instruments like the oboe and cor anglais whose nasal timbre matches that of muted brass very well indeed when the brass players possess a good ear for blend and tone-colour, but it is from the muted horn that we can expect the most poetic and evocative sounds when it is played softly and well in tune.

The mute is less frequently applied to the tuba. It muffles the tone but does not produce the characteristically nasal timbre of the other muted brass instruments.

E

CHAPTER V

PERCUSSION — HARP AND PIANOFORTE

THE TIMPANI (kettledrums) hold pride of place among percussion instruments, most of which are incapable of producing notes of definite pitch. Up to and including the classical period two drums were used. They were tuned to the tonic and dominant. Originally the timpani part was written always on C and G, the tuning being indicated at the beginning of the piece thus:

But it later ceased to be a transposing instrument probably because it was found useful to be able to give the tonic to the lower drum and the dominant to the higher in certain keys owing to the limited pitch-range or compass of each individual drum, e.g. :

Beethoven in his Eighth and Ninth Symphonies tunes his drums in high and low F, so that the transposing system would have been still more meaningless for this tuning.

Before long a third drum was added. This was intermediate between the high and low drum. In this way the subdominant could be added to the tonic and dominant and composers soon realised that any tuning which suited the piece in hand and was available on the three drums could be used, and also that the tuning of any or all the drums could be changed in the course of a movement if sufficient rests were given for this to be carried out.

Tuning is effected by means of seven tuning handles, one of which, facing the player, is detachable so as not to interfere with his movements from one drum to another. These handles work on screws attached to a rim which presses down on the edge of the head (parchment) tightening it uniformly all the way round. Changes of tuning involving only a semitone or tone can be managed quite quickly. The player knows exactly what fraction of a turn is required. If the change is of a large interval he needs more time and the tuning may not be absolutely right until the drum has been struck in its new tuning and then slightly adjusted. Good drummers develop a very fine ear for pitch, and in fact need to be first-class musicians in every way. They usually possess several pairs of sticks of varying hardness from which they select the pair most suited to the matter in hand. Kettledrum parts are written at their sounded pitch. It has been established by scientific experiment that a kettledrum is really sounding its second harmonic, the octave from its fundamental note. When two drums are used their pitch-limits are roughly these :

Ex:29

The lower drum can however give a fairly good low E and even E flat and the higher can go up to F sharp or G, though these latter tunings put some strain on the head.

When a third drum is used it stands in pitch between these two, say from G up to E flat. The tighter the drum is screwed up the more definite and clear is the pitch. The tuning A and D on the two outer drums is particularly good, the head being reasonably stretched—not too much to impair resonance, but tight enough to give a clear ringing note. The low notes are however by no means to be avoided especially in music of a solemn character.

In modern scores the reader will find that the notes of the timpani part are changed rapidly and without warning. This is because the composer has mechanically tuned, or "machine drums" in mind. These instruments are more common abroad than in these islands. The tuning is done by tightening and loosening the rim by means of a pedal mechanism. As well as enabling re-tuning to be instantaneous, the machine drum can be used for glissando rolls. Bartok used this effect in his Sonata for two pianos and percussion, and one also occurs in his Concerto for Orchestra. Walford Davies also wrote glissandi in a symphony written quite early in this century and no doubt many other composers have done so. This is, of course, a special effect to be used sparingly. In order to cope with modern drum parts written for machine drums, the drummer who prefers to play the hand-tuned types needs five or six drums and has to go over the part very carefully, marking in all necessary re-tunings.

It is advisable if a part is written for machine drums to provide an alternative simplified part for three hand-tuned drums. In heavily scored works two or even more timpanists are written for. Berlioz writes chords to be played by four drums rolling in his *Symphonie Fantastique* and Holst employs two sets of three drums in *The Planets* so tuned that in *Jupiter* and *Uranus* they can be used thematically. In this respect he has been forestalled by Wagner who wrote for two pairs of timpani in the *Ring* and *Parsifal,* and exploited their possibilities to the full.

The timpani can execute rhythmical figures of considerable complexity and rapidity either on a single drum or divided between two or three and are effective when used in this way at all dynamic levels. The duration of notes should be written exactly especially in quiet passages. In loud passages where most or

THE ELEMENTS OF ORCHESTRATION 69

all of the orchestra is playing this does not matter very much as the resonance of the drums is obscured by the general loudness of sound that is going on. But in soft passages this resonance or sustaining power should be taken into account. If short notes are written the player will damp the note with his hand so if a more spacious effect is wanted minims or semibreves or whatever are required should be written.

The roll is executed by striking the drum rapidly and with equal force with the sticks alternately. It can be used at all dynamic levels but a long roll of several bars' duration fortissimo is very tiring for the player. Piano and pianissimo rolls can proceed for virtually unlimited periods without unduly exhausting the player though they need control to keep the beating perfectly even with no " hills or valleys " in the tone. The roll need not end with a final strike unless this is particularly desired. Crescendo and diminuendo rolls are of course both possible and effective.

The timpani should never be used unless its tuning allows it to have a note of the harmony at any given point. The bass of the chord is naturally the best note for it to have, but failing this any note of the chord will do. The only exception to this would be the use of an unrelated drum note on a short, sharp and loud bang on the full orchestra. This would be immediately damped by the player and there would not be time for the ear to detect the discrepancy of pitch. It should be added that instances of this are very rare and one would not recommend it as a general practice. The tuning of the drums is, or should be, very exact and it is a great mistake to regard it as merely approximate.

A timpanist must be a good musician and should always read the score of a work in which he is going to perform if he can get hold of it so as to be able to judge the relationship of his part to the total effect. A conductor is always thankful for the presence of a really reliable and intelligent timpanist. His part in the orchestra is so telling and individual, especially in modern works, that he is looked upon as an important soloist in the orchestra and one who can contribute both rhythmical firmness and dramatic excitement to an interpretation.

In the classical symphonic orchestra it was a rare event when any percussion instruments apart from the timpani were used. In the opera house where the music has often to be highly coloured, even flamboyant, percussion instruments were of much more frequent appearance. Bass drum, cymbals and triangle were known collectively in the eighteenth century as "Turkish Music" and it was these instruments that Haydn used in his *Military Symphony* and Beethoven in the finale of No. 9. As drama and excitement entered the concert hall from the theatre the percussion department became a normal constituent of the symphony orchestra and other instruments came to be used as well as the conventional "Turkish Music". The side drum was brought in from the barrack square and its crisp crackle was found to be splendid not only in music of a military cast but as an additional and powerful adjunct to strongly rhythmical passages. Bells, gongs, glockenspiel, xylophone and the rest were called upon to give picturesque or local colour. Recently, many of these instruments, including celesta and vibraphone, have come to be used as important solo instruments instead of merely adding extra colour to the normal orchestral ensemble.

The percussion department has thus progressed a long way since the time when it was rather slightingly termed "the kitchen" by orchestral musicians. It includes within its scope not only instruments which boom, crash, tinkle and crackle on notes of indefinite pitch, but many others of delicacy and refinement which can produce notes over quite a wide range of pitch, and the orchestra has been invaded lately by exotic and colourful percussion instruments from Latin America and elsewhere. These are used not so much to evoke local colour as for their own sakes as contributors of sounds which are fresh to frequenters of symphony concerts, but will probably not be so for very much longer.

The parts of percussion instruments which have no definite pitch are written and printed either on conventional notes in either treble or bass clefs according to whether their sound is high or low, or on single lines. The latter method saves space in the score especially when four or five percussion players are employed. A handy and compendious example of this notation can be seen on pages 48 and 49 of the miniature score of Britten's *Variations and Fugue on a Theme of Henry Purcell*, otherwise known as *The Young Person's Guide to the Orchestra*. Here we

see parts for Whip, Triangle, Gong, Cymbals, Bass Drum, Castanets and Side Drum, each printed on a single line without clefs
(Boosey and Hawkes Ltd.). If a complete staff of five lines is
allotted to one of these instruments the Whip, Triangle, Cymbals,
Castanets and Side Drum would be written with treble clefs either
all on C, third space or, if differentiation to the eye were thought
desirable, perhaps on the D above this C, C, B, A and G respectively. The Bass Drum would be written in the Bass clef on C,
second space, and the Gong either on that same note or another
in the bass clef, say G on the bottom line.

Orchestras cannot often afford armies of percussion like this,
and sometimes only one player apart from timpani is available,
and very often not more than two.

In this case plenty of colour and variety can be obtained if
the available player or players are given time to change from one
instrument to another. Professional percussion players can be
relied on to provide and play all the normal instruments both
of definite and indefinite pitch, but it is wise to limit one's enthusiasm to some extent in the interests of space in the orchestra
(it is disturbing even if there is plenty of room to have players
constantly walking from one large instrument to another) and
also practicability in transport. One does not want to have to
charter a pantechnicon for the sake of one or two effects, however cherished.

When writing for amateurs one must be prepared for
omissions in equipment and it is wise only to write for quite
normal things or to be resigned to the fact that any less ordinary
ones may have to be regarded as " ad lib ". School orchestras
are often quite rich in both percussion players and instruments
and with them one need not necessarily be prepared for many
disappointments of this kind, even if in other departments they
may have deficiencies. The normal instruments without definite
pitch may be said to be Bass Drum, Cymbals, Side Drum,
Triangle and Tambourine.

The instruments with definite pitch include as above mentioned the Glockenspiel, in which steel bars are struck by
hammers, the Xylophone which has wooden bars instead of the
Glockenspiel's metal ones, the Celesta which resembles the
Glockenspiel in that the sound is produced by hammers striking

metal bars, but the hammers are here actuated by a piano keyboard. The tone is usually more fruity and resonant than that of the Glockenspiel, but these instruments appear to vary a good deal in quality and musicality of tone just as do Triangles and other percussion instruments. Tubular Bells are commonly used, mostly for realistic bell effects, but single strokes can produce subtly emotional results when used against a well chosen background. Cf. Webern's *Six Orchestral Pieces* Op. 6. In Hindemith's *Metamorphosis of themes of Weber No. 2*, fine use is made of a percussion ensemble, consisting of four Timpani, Tubular Bells (" Chimes "), Triangle, Tom-tom, Wood-block, Small Cymbal and Small Gong.

An instrument which has recently been imported into the symphony orchestra from the dance band is the vibraphone. This is played by striking steel bars with hammers, and thus is related to the Glockenspiel. Its sound is prevented from dying away quickly by means of resonators and an electrical device which also gives the notes a continual vibrato. The sound can be cut off by dampers worked by a pedal. Vaughan Williams used the vibraphone in his eighth symphony and Walton in his second. It also appears in scores by Berg, Messiaen and a number of recent composers. Single notes and chords up to eight notes can be played and sustained for a considerable time, the rate of vibrato being controlled by the speed of the electric motor.

The harp defies classification in any of the four orchestral groups. It is of course a stringed instrument but the " Strings " have come to connote for musicians the instruments of the violin family. Harp music is written on two staves like that for the piano. The strings are plucked by the thumb and first three fingers of each hand. The little finger is not used, so not more than four-note chords can be played by each hand. In order to provide a large range of notes, approximating to the compass of the piano, it is impossible to construct a chromatically tuned harp which is really satisfactory because of the limited length of the human arm. The harp in universal use today is the double action harp invented by Sebastian Erard. Each string can be made to sound the flat, natural and sharp forms of its note, the natural and sharp inflections are obtained by seven pedals, one for each note of the diatonic scale. When a pedal is pressed down and secured by the first notch all the strings bearing the same letter-name are raised a semitone and become naturals. The second notch raises them another semitone to sharps. Since every note of the scale has to be flat before it can be raised to natural and sharp it follows that the harp has to be tuned to the scale of C flat. The right foot has four pedals to operate, the left foot three. The notes (or strings) affected by the right pedals are E, F, G and A; the left pedals dealing with B, C and D. The harp is designed essentially for diatonic music. Chromatic harmony and melody have to be written with great care for it if impossibly quick pedal changes are to be avoided. A good deal of this sort of trouble can be circumvented by the use of enharmonic notes, D flat instead of C sharp and so on. Enharmonic tuning also makes possible the setting of the harp in a considerable variety of scales and arpeggios for use mainly in glissandi. For instance diminished seventh chords can all be set, e.g. B sharp, C natural, D sharp, E flat, F sharp, G flat and A. The repetition of the enharmonic notes is not audible as such in rapid glissandi. Other chords of the seventh, both dominant and secondary can also be set, but not all, as the reader will find if he tries to find a " glissando " tuning for chords which contain a preponderance of white notes on the piano. For instance the dominant seventh of C is ruled out because no harmony note can be obtained from the A string. Pentatonic scales on both " white " and " black " notes are perfectly feasible with the following tunings : F, G, A, B sharp, C, D, E sharp (white notes) and F sharp, G sharp, A sharp, B flat, C sharp, D sharp and E flat (black notes) and both of the whole tone scales, those on C and C sharp are equally possible. The harp glissando has become a cliché through over-use as an " exciting " effect in popular music, but as a murmurous background in quiet passages it is still highly effective, repeatedly moving up and down a scale or chord. Glissandi can be played with both hands at once in octaves or at any other interval. They can also be played in chords. It is not necessary to write all the notes of a glissando passage. If the tuning is clearly indicated either by key-signature or otherwise the glissando is indicated by lines joining the top and bottom notes, or sometimes the first octave is written out with any necessary chromatic alterations shown. The

first method is recommended. Life is too short to write down any
unnecessary notes. It is advisable to give the first note the time
value of the whole glissando to make sure of obtaining the
required timing. Here are some examples of the notation :

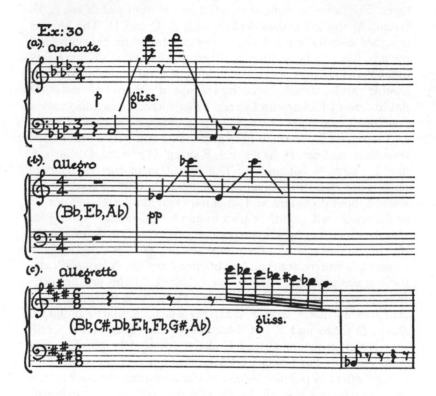

Ex: 30

(a). andante

(b). allegro

(Bb, Eb, Ab)

(c). allegretto

(Bb, C#, Db, E♮, Fb, G#, Ab)   gliss.

Chords on the harp are slightly spread or rolled unless instructions are given to the contrary. For good sonority the hands
should not be far apart. Arpeggios (the word is derived from
Arpa = Harp) of course suit its nature excellently. The deepest
notes of the instrument are best doubled at the octave above and
enharmonic unisons help to give them substance :

Low octave passages are sometimes used to give a slight attack or ictus to passages for 'cellos and basses.

Harp harmonics are obtained by touching a string at its central point. When plucked it vibrates in two halves and gives the octave above the normal note. The quality of sound is attractive and romantic. It is useless to try to describe the sounds of instruments. They must be heard and stored in the memory. The notation of harmonics is shown here:

Chords in harmonics of three notes can be played by the left hand but only single notes with the right.

The strings in their original flat position are more resonant than when they are raised by the pedals. It is therefore advisable to write flats rather than sharps both in single notes and chords. That is why one finds composers writing their harp parts in the keys of C flat or G flat when the rest of the orchestra may be playing in the enharmonically equivalent keys of B or F sharp. A short example of this may be found in Bartok's Concerto for Orchestra (fig. 256 in the Finale) where the two harps play a passage in the key of C flat while the divided violins play with sharp notation in the key of B.

Composers in recent times have taken to including the pianoforte in their orchestral works not as a solo instrument, though it may be given solo passages, but for the sake of its brilliance in its top octaves and the sonority of its low notes. From the orchestral point of view there is less value to be had from the normal middle range of the piano, admirable though this is in solo work. In using the pianoforte as an orchestral instrument the aim should be to use it in such a way that it does not " sound like a pianoforte ", but as a powerful and highly characterised addition to the percussion department and a companion in some ways too for the harp. Harp and pianoforte figuration interweaving in high registers could be a fine addition to the orchestral palette and fat chords at the bottom of the piano go well with low percussion instruments such as Timpani, Bass Drum and Gong.

The pianoforte is, of course, much used to fill in the parts of missing instruments in incomplete orchestras. Commercial orchestrations are often made with " piano-conductor " parts which contain all the elements of the work, melody and harmony with indications of the instrumentation. In theory at least the piano-conductor might be said to take the place of the continuo player who directed performances from his seat at the harpsichord in the eighteenth century, but the artistic value of an orchestration cued down to the limit and making provision for the possible absence of practically the entire orchestra cannot be very great. It does happen that circumstances may arise which render cueing down necessary, especially in the case of school and amateur orchestras, and later in this book I intend to devote considerable space to this matter.

THE SAXOPHONES

The Saxophones form a complete family of instruments, sopranino, soprano, alto, tenor, baritone and bass. They do not belong to the orchestra's normal specification but composers have written for them, and if they had not been captured by dance-bands they might have become regular members, more or less, of the symphony orchestra. Their chief use is as solo instruments, the E flat alto saxophone being the most frequently used and after that the tenor in B flat or C. The sopranino (as used by Ravel in his *Bolero*) is in F and is a rare instrument, but all the others are either in B flat or E flat and are written for in the treble clef. The B flat soprano sounds a tone down, the E flat alto a major sixth down, the B flat tenor a ninth down, the E flat baritone a major sixth plus an octave down and the B flat bass a ninth plus an octave down.

Thus the transpositions work as follows:—

Ex:33

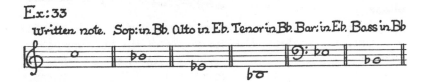

The most frequently used forms of saxophones are the alto in E flat and the tenor in B flat. Apart from their use in dance bands these two saxophones have established themselves as an integral part of the Military Band.

Saxophones are mentioned here because they may sometimes be used in school or amateur orchestras as substitutes for horns. But the general style of playing with its overdone vibrato and frequent disregard for niceties of intonation makes it something of a risk to write for this instrument. Berlioz in his treatise on orchestration, written when the saxophone was a new invention, said prophetically that it would probably be put to uses then un-dreamed of. Wagner rejected saxophones because of their un-satisfactory blend with the wind instruments of the orchestra. It is this which has kept them out of symphonic music except for rare appearances as solo instruments, where ability to stand out against a background is a virtue and blending is not required. When the saxophone is played by an artist its tone is pleasing, though not very pure in timbre. It sounds rather like mixtures of other instruments, bassoon, clarinet and horn. But its melancholy sound suits well such solos as Ravel and Vaughan Williams gave it in Moussorgsky's *Castle in Spain* from *Pictures from an Exhibition* (orchestrated by Ravel) and *" Job "* respectively. Debussy wrote a concerto for saxophone; Bizet, Massenet and other French composers used it in some of their operas and Richard Strauss used a quartet of saxophones in his *Sinfonia Domestica*. But it has found its true *métier* in jazz and its association with that highly individual and idiomatic branch of music has done most to bar it from anything approaching regular membership of the orchestra. Berg, by the way, alternates his third clarinet in his Violin Concerto with Alto E flat Saxophone. The reeds and mouthpieces of saxophone and clarinet are almost identical and any clarinettist can quickly learn to play the saxophone.

This completes our brief review of the various orchestral instruments and sections. The compasses of the instruments are given all together in Chapter XII (p. 196) for easy reference. These should be committed to memory so that they become after a little while inseparably connected with the instruments in the mind of the orchestrator. Without a clear conception of the ranges at which the instruments, at any rate those in common use, are effective and comfortable to play and an absolutely infallible grasp of their upper and lower limits of pitch, little progress can be made.

Information as to the techniques of fingering, tone production and the actual construction of instruments can be found in varying degrees of completeness in larger treatises on instrumentation and in the articles of Grove's Dictionary which deal with the separate instruments.

Ability to play some of the instruments is of course a tremendous help in writing for them, but it is not essential, in fact the possession of inadequate technical prowess as a performer may be inhibiting in writing for an instrument. One has only to think of Berlioz, whose ability to play any instrument at all was practically non-existent, if one wants reassurance in this matter. Demonstrations by good players or even chance remarks from them can be very illuminating and all hints derived from such sources as instrumental "tutors" and books of studies, scores and so on should be looked upon as bricks to be used in building up what one hopes will eventually become an imposing edifice of really practical technical knowledge enabling one to write with confidence for any available combination, great or small.

PART II
PRACTICE

F

CHAPTER VI

THE SMALL CLASSICAL ORCHESTRA

However large an orchestra a composer uses, by far the greatest amount of work will be done by Strings, Woodwind and Horns. Trumpets, Trombones, Tuba, Harp and Percussion (excluding Timpani) are reserved chiefly for building up or adding weight to climaxes or for special colouristic effects (in the case of the harp and the light percussion).

Some figures in this connection are interesting. Elgar's *Enigma* Variations consist of the Theme and fourteen Variations. The brass (excluding horns) are not used at all in the Theme or in Variations II, VI, VIII, X, and XII. In Variation I they play in eight bars out of twenty-two, in Variation III the trumpets play in four bars out of thirty-five, in Variation V in five bars out of twenty-four, and in Variation XIII in seven bars out of fifty-one. Even in the *Nimrod* Variation, which is so rich in texture, the brass do not enter until the twenty-seventh bar and there are only forty-three bars altogether, the last two bars containing no brass. We can therefore say that in two-thirds of the fifteen sections the brass are either not used at all or are only sparingly employed. As for percussion apart from Timpani the two players (or three if separate performers are used for bass drum and cymbals) are only required in three movements and have little to do except in the Finale.

The Finale of Bartok's Concerto for Orchestra, a movement full of colour, vivacity and robustness, is six-hundred-and-twenty-five bars long. Out of these the brass play in two-hundred-and-thirty. In the Finale of Walton's First Symphony, again a most

83

full-blooded movement, the brass play in two-hundred-and-fifteen bars out of five-hundred-and-twenty-three. These three examples were taken at random with no previous idea of what results they would yield.

It is clear then that even in fully scored works the heavy brass are silent for well over half of the time. This brings us to the point that the woodwind, horns and strings have most of the work and that the handling of this combination is the essential and fundamental requirement in the acquisition of a good technique in orchestration.

One of the smallest orchestras to be used in a full-scale symphonic masterpiece is that employed by Mozart in the original version of his G Minor Symphony (K.550). Only seven wind instruments appear in the score and they are Flute, two Oboes, two Bassoons and two Horns. There were two later versions, one with Clarinets substituted for Oboes and another with Clarinets added to the original version, the Oboe parts being modified to suit this arrangement.

I wish now to go through the first movement in some detail, but before proceeding any further the reader might try his hand at orchestrating it himself from a pianoforte or, better, a pianoforte duet version and compare it with Mozart's score. Exactly the same instruments, including the two Horns (natural Horns, of course) in different keys, B flat, alto and G. The 'cellos and basses can be written on one stave (in unison to the eye, but in octaves to the ear) as Mozart yokes them together all through the movement except for one brief passage.

In order to derive any benefit from what follows the reader needs a score of the original version and must number every tenth bar for ease of reference.

Let us first consider the two Horn parts and find out what notes are available from the Harmonic Series based on G and B flat starting with the second harmonic, the fundamental being practically useless, and ending with the twelfth harmonic, this being a sensible upward limit for these relatively short and high pitched Horns. The written series of notes, we remember are :

Ex:34

On the B flat alto horn these notes will sound a tone lower, and on the G horn they will sound a fourth lower. The sounds available from the two horns together are therefore :

Ex:35

We find that the 6th, 7th, 11th and 12th harmonics of the G Horn are identical with the 5th, 6th and 9th and 10th of the B flat, but all the same a considerable variety of notes is available. The 7th harmonics are out of tune and are placed within brackets. Useful notes in the keys of G minor, B flat major and G major all appear in the above series, thus making it very valuable in a G minor movement. For the sake of those who propose to orchestrate this movement it is fair to point out that Mozart's Horn parts do not go above the 10th harmonic. The G Horn descends to the 3rd harmonic but the B flat horn does not go below the fourth.

We may now proceed with our examination of Mozart's score. The first thing to notice is the viola writing in the first thirteen bars. Although the sign " div." is not given, this passage is to be played by divided violas. In classical works " div." is not always inserted. It is usually obvious whether division or double stops are intended by the composer. This independent use of the violas to provide the whole of the inner harmony is unusual for the period. We shall see that Mozart reverts to the practice of using the violas to reinforce the bass line an octave higher in many places. In passing we notice that the fifth (D) of the G Minor chord is omitted from the opening bars of the viola parts

so as not to interfere with the free interplay of E flat and D in
the violin melody. At bar fourteen the little woodwind phrase is
given to flute, oboe and bassoon, a favourite tone-colour of
Mozart's, and the ensuing forte wind chords are laid out in such
a way as to get clarity and strength. All the instruments are playing fairly high, not uncomfortably so, and are able to hold their
own perfectly against the powerful unison of the strings. In bars
twenty and twenty-one, the thirds on the two bassoons provide
an unobtrusive support to the violins. Bars twenty-two and
twenty-seven provide an excellent example of the use of wind instruments in harmony to give stability to the string texture. This
passage also shows Mozart's exquisitely sensitive musicality in
drawing attention to the change in harmony and tonality from
that at the opening statement of the subject.

At bar twenty-eight begins an energetic *tutti* in the relative
major. The B flat horn can be used here extensively. The G horn
contributes what he can, which is not very much, though he can
and does add weight and fullness just where it is needed at an
important change of harmony. In this *tutti* flute and oboes reinforce and sustain the violin notes on the first beat of each bar.
The bassoons double the busy bass part and the violas play a
" mirror " version of it in the higher octave. The second violins
mostly play in unison or octaves with the firsts, but break into an
independent part for the last five bars of the passage. Bar forty-
four brings us to the second subject. Note how the first phrase is
rounded off by oboe and bassoon and how the violins are carried
over to the E flat so as to ensure a smooth join between the two
contrasted tone-colours. At bar fifty-two, wind and strings change
places, and join forces at bar fifty-eight. This charmingly scored
passage is of deceptive simplicity. The notes are so well placed
that there would seem to be no other way of setting them out.

At bar seventy note the use, another favourite one of the composer, of flute, violins and bassoons in a triple octave combination. In the five bars beginning at bar seventy-two the little piece
of canonic imitation between the first violins and the basses is en-
riched by the fourth string of the violas reinforcing the bass line
in situ and not at the octave above. After this they are written an
octave above the basses up to the end of the exposition. At bars
seventy-seven to eighty and subsequent similar passages the flute

and oboe are placed high for brilliance and the second violins add richness and vigour to the ensemble with their very easily executed double-stops and their doublings of the first violins at the sixth, the unison and the octave. The horns again play what they can, the G horn being rather starved for possible notes in the prevailing tonality of B flat major. I would like here to urge the reader not to skimp anything in reading a score. It is easy to observe rather lazily that the horns are playing, but it is important to a full appreciation of Mozart's skill and resourcefulness to take the trouble to work out what actual notes they are playing. The passage in double thirds at bar one-hundred-and-two reminds us of the bassoons at bar twenty and the cohesive effect of the same instruments in the passage beginning at bar one-hundred-and-seven, with the second bassoon sustaining the bass, should not go unnoticed. Such quiet wind backgrounds as this play the part of a sustaining pedal in the orchestra. Students in their early stages rarely seem to grasp the importance of these effects because when they listen they take them for granted. Indeed the composer does not want them to be noticed consciously but merely felt as an enrichment of the score and as a means of correcting any scratchiness (less rare no doubt in Mozart's day than ours) that may emanate from the string section. At bar one-hundred-and-fourteen the contrapuntal development of the principal subjects begins. Here it is most important that the bass line be clearly and strongly articulated. The violas double the 'cellos in unison except where the bass line would lead them out of their depth. The bassoons also reinforce the bass. The violins play sometimes in unison, sometimes in octaves. Flute and oboe supply the dissonant element which adds tensile strength to the texture by means of suspensions, and the horns find themselves able to contribute notes in spite of the modulations that are taking place. The G horn finds a use for his major third at bar one-hundred-and-fifteen, and this helps greatly to amplify the bass entry at this point. At bar one-hundred-and-thirty-eight begins the beautiful passage based on the opening notes of the principal subjects and which leads eventually to the recapitulation. At bar one-hundred-and-forty observe the unison doubling of second oboe and first bassoon. Mozart was evidently afraid that the bassoon alone would be too thin in tone and too weak to support the texture adequately. It is interesting to note that in the version with clarinets added the oboe parts are here transferred to clarinets whose smooth tone blends better with flute and bassoon than the oboes do in a quiet passage like this. From bar one-hundred-and-forty-six to one-hundred-and-fifty-two the 'cellos enjoy their brief respite from their constant companions the double basses. Bars one-hundred-and-fifty-three to one-hundred-and-fifty-nine make a splendid sound which makes it difficult to believe that so few instruments are employed. The sforzando horns, the high-placed 'cellos and basses (basses are very powerful at this pitch) the woodwind chords folding and unfolding and the interjections from the upper strings all combine in a wonderfully integrated way to produce a feeling of expectancy. But the return of the first subject is postponed by the delicious little woodwind passage from bar one-hundred-and-sixty to one-hundred-and-sixty-six. Note how the horns take over the pedal D from the bassoons when the latter are wanted elsewhere.

The recapitulation starts normally with a restatement of the first subject scored as before for strings, but the bassoon joins in with a very simple but effective counterpoint at bar one-hundred-and-sixty-eight. A little point worth noting occurs at bar one-hundred-and-eighty-nine where instead of taking the violins up to F and continuing at that high pitch until bar one-hundred-and-ninety-one, Mozart drops them to B flat and can thus neatly continue in the lower octave. The higher octave is resumed at bar one-hundred-and-ninety-two by leaping up a fifth instead of down a fourth (as in the exposition). All this was done to avoid a rather awkward scoop up from A flat to F in bar one-hundred-and-eighty-nine, and provides an example of a little piece of admirable craftsmanship. At bar one-hundred-and-ninety-eight, where the chief interest is transferred to the bass, bassoons and violas join the 'cellos and basses. The violins supply the brilliance and the woodwind and horns the harmonic basis, as is so often their role. From bars two-hundred-and-three to two-hundred-and-twelve, both horns are able to play continuously, being able to produce from their scanty store notes germane to the harmony. The second subject (bar two-hundred-and-twenty-seven) is scored almost as it is in the exposition, but the little wind interjections are brightened by the higher octave on the flute, and bassoon and flute double the violins above and below at bar two-hundred-and-thirty-nine. There are also changes in the harmony and lay-out of the wind parts in bars two-hundred-and-thirty-five to two-hundred-and-thirty-eight. At bar two-hundred-and-forty-seven and succeeding bars note the triple-octave combination of flute, oboe and bassoon to balance the powerful string parts. In bars two-hundred-and-sixty to two-hundred-and-seventy-two the contrasts obtainable from such small resources are shown in the little woodwind figure, first on oboe, then on bassoon, then on flute and oboe in octaves and then on two bassoons in octaves with a different order adopted the second time the passage comes, when sustained horn notes give added sonority. Bars two-hundred-and-eighty-one to two-hundred-and-eighty-four furnish a fine example of how the strings with their nervous excitable temperament can give point to a passage which might otherwise be rather dull. Bars two-hundred-and-eighty-seven to two-hundred-and-eighty-nine do not sound thin because of the rhythmic contrasts between the three contrapuntal parts. The distance between the second violins and the bass allows the violas to come in with their little figure without room having to be made for them. This passage of six bars from two-hundred-and-eighty-seven is beautifully contrived both harmonically and in instrumentation.

A few bars later this wonderful movement comes to an end. What lessons have we learned from it? Some answers to this question follow :

(1) Independence of Wind and String parts. There is very little exact doubling of Wind and Strings except when the bassoons reinforce the bass line when it is thematically important or the violins are doubled by a Wind instrument an octave higher (usually the flute) or lower (usually the bassoon). The Wind may sometimes play a simplified version of the String parts.

(2) The Wind parts are less active on the whole than the Strings which are mobile and restless by nature. The Wind and Horns very often supply the harmonic basis, sometimes with sustained, sometimes with rhythmically repeated, chords.

(3) It is possible to write effective horn parts even when

available notes are restricted to those of the Harmonic series, but Mozart often had to leave out the Horns where he would have liked to have them in loud passages. Quiet held notes, particularly in octaves on two Horns, greatly help in adding smoothness and depth to the texture. Although modern Horn writing is very much freer than Mozart's could possibly have been it is very good discipline and a challenge to ingenuity to write for natural Horns as an exercise.

(4) Single Woodwind instruments are not powerful enough by themselves to vie with energetic string writing when used contrapuntally against them. A triple octave combination is needed for this rather than strengthening the tonal power by unison doubling.

(5) Normal Flute writing in the orchestra lies rather high (mostly from F, top line, to G the ninth above). The Flute's principal function is to supply top notes to wind chords or to double melodies on other instruments at the higher octave. It is, in fact, a " four-foot " instrument most of the time. In the eighteenth century the low notes were of poor quality and not well in tune. They can be freely used now but are of weak penetrating power. Composers still, quite rightly, think of the flute chiefly as a high-pitched instrument, but far less exclusively than they did in Mozart's day.

(6) The Second Violins very frequently double the First an octave lower and not seldom in actual unison in brilliant passages. They may too, of course, fill in the harmony sometimes using simple double-stops.

(7) The Violas may have an independent part but often reinforce the bass, sometimes in unison with the 'cellos, sometimes an octave higher. They may also double the second violins in unison if the passage lies fairly low. The Viola has gained enormously in prestige since Mozart's time, and far more is expected of this section of the Strings now than then.

(8) 'Cellos and Basses playing together in octave supply a perfectly strong bass to a super-structure of woodwind, horns and upper strings. The bassoons can therefore be free to

play inner parts in the tenor register unless, as we have mentioned above, a particularly strong bass line is desired.

(9) It is highly important to indicate the style in which any passage is to be played by means of bowing-slurs for strings or phrasing-slurs for wind or their absence, staccato dots, sforzando marks, dynamics and so on. Nothing must be left to chance in these ways.

(10) The String section plays almost continuously. Passages for Strings alone far exceed in number those for Wind alone. String tone is homogeneous throughout the whole family of instruments and thus forms a perfect basis on which to build orchestral textures. The ear tires of unbroken wind tone much quicker than of the sound of strings.

In the light of later developments in orchestral writing some of the above principles have to be modified but most of them remain true today.

Let us now look at the score of Mendelssohn's *Fingal's Cave* Overture. This is no doubt familiar to the reader, but he may not have examined it in detail. Over forty years separates this from Mozart's G minor Symphony and we may therefore expect to find in it some modifications and expansions of orchestral technique. In the first place, although woodwind and horns carry most of the burden in the wind department, Mendelssohn uses trumpet and timpani in addition as well as a larger woodwind section than the meagre one which Mozart allowed himself in the symphony. Mendelssohn's orchestra was, however, the standard symphonic orchestra used by Mozart, Haydn and Beethoven in most of their orchestral works and therefore the actual size of the orchestra is no larger than what had been normal for over half a century. Mendelssohn's horns and trumpets are without valves, like Mozart's, and he therefore suffered under the same disadvantages as his illustrious predecessors in this way. I have chosen this work because it is well known to all music lovers and because it is the work of one of the finest orchestral craftsmen of all time.

We note that Mendelssohn chooses clarinets in A which gives them a simple key to play in, and that his horns and trumpets are in D which of course gives him a considerable number of notes in B minor including its dominant but not its tonic. The 'cellos and basses are written on separate staves because they play independently at times instead of practically always playing in octaves. The timpani are tuned to the customary tonic and dominant, B and F sharp (low).

At the beginning the main theme is given to the 'cellos and first bassoon, with the violas an octave above. This ensures that, though low in pitch, it dominates the scene. In the third and fourth bars the 'cellos leave the theme and play an accompanying part but after that they rejoin the bassoons and violas. The way the chords are built up by the violins and woodwind is to be noted. Mendelssohn was always inclined to write his second flute rather low and so he makes it come in on low D sharp two octaves below the first instead of one octave. The second violins are looking after the D sharp above and so no weakness results. As the structure becomes more weighty with the addition of the pairs of woodwind instruments one after the other the second bassoon is made to help the double basses at the sixth bar. At bar nine the main melody passes to the violins in octaves, the 'cellos and violas supplying a semiquaver counterpoint. Horns and trumpets play the same role as the violins and upper woodwind did in the opening bars. In bars thirteen and fourteen the bassoons virtually become horns, playing in between the held horn F sharps. The timpani here help the double basses with the bass line. At bar fifteen note the double bass simplification of the 'cello part. The whole of the first twenty-four bars of the overture provide a good illustration of the principle of active strings against a sustained background of wind. At bar twenty-four the basses descend to D. This is a note below the bottom note of the normally tuned four-stringed bass and a fourth below the three-stringer which was commonly used at that time (tuned in fifths to G D and A). Such notes were frequently written (but more especially when the 'cellos and basses were written together on the same staff because the 'cellos could go down to C) but had to be played an octave higher as they are today except by possessors of five-string basses or of four-stringers with unconventional tuning. From bars twenty-six to thirty we see the familiar classical triple octave combination of flute, oboe and bassoon. Quiet held notes on horns and trumpets enrich the texture here and in passing we may notice the crescendo and decrescendo signs which had come into musical notation since Mozart's day. At bar thirty-seven sharpened forms of the ninth and eleventh harmonics are used on the horns, but Mendelssohn does not risk them on the trumpets which would have to trust to overblowing the natural notes whereas the horns can get them by hand-stopping. The trumpets come in at bar forty-five softly yet decidedly, sounding A in preparation for the D major of the second subject at bar forty-seven. Here the upper strings keep up their fluid, wavy motion while 'cellos and bassoons play the tune. Note that the upper strings are marked *pp*, the basses *p* and the 'cellos and bassoons *mf*. The rich tones of the clarinets in their chalumeau register are added to the melody when it comes within their range and the flutes add a delightful touch of colour at bar forty-nine and a few bars later also.

When the violins take up the melody at bar fifty-seven they are marked *mf* against the *pp* of the lower strings. During the next ten bars the less obtrusive wind instruments, horns, clarinets and bassoons in turn are used, also marked *pp* to give cohesion to the harmonics underlying the figuration of the viola and 'cello parts. In bars sixty-seven to seventy-three note the wide spacing of the string parts which gives a limpid, transparent background to the flutes. The lay-out of the whole of this passage as far as the *ff* at bar seventy-seven (letter B) will repay study. Note in particular the rich sound of the trumpets and the effect of their crescendo. Where they enter, Mendelssohn takes his second flute off the melodic line and uses the more powerful clarinet instead. Note also the very effective entry of the oboes in octaves and the way they bite into the smooth texture. At B the rhythm of the dominating motif of the piece is slightly altered and thereby gains power and urgency. This rhythm is underlined by the horns and trumpets. One would expect the violas to double the bass part as they do at bar eighty-one, but instead they are silent for three bars. Perhaps Mendelssohn wanted to add a little something more to the bass figure where the violins go higher, and saved up the violas for this. The whole of this *tutti* is splendidly written for the orchestra. A point to be particularly admired is the way the strings are used in bars eighty-nine to ninety-two with the violins and violas on their fourth strings surging and frothing beneath the high-placed full chords on the wind. In bars ninety-six to ninety-eight, note the way the violas, 'cellos and basses handle their descending arpeggio crotchets, overlapping well so as to make smooth the take-overs. In bars one-hundred to one-hundred-and-two there is a slight change. By remaining on the B and moving from that note down to E the 'cellos are able to give distinctness of pitch to the the basses' bottom note (also Mendelssohn may have been aware of the limitations of pitch of the three-stringed bass which would have to come up to the final E. In this event the 'cellos would give the illusion of descent to the final note). We have drawn attention to the use of the woodwind in this passage early in the book. The interjections on trumpets and horns are very effective and must have surprised early audiences of the work. In passing it is interesting, and illuminating too, to recall that some critics supposed that Mr. Mendelssohn knew what he was after, but this overture would take a lot of getting used to, or words to that effect. The string writing in the passage beginning at bar one-hundred-and-twenty-three is subtle in spite of its simplicity to sophisticated ears and eyes. Putting the 'cellos above the violas so as to exploit the expressive power of the 'cellos' top string was then a novel idea, if not actually unprecedented, and has been much done since. It is nice too the way the violas go between the violins when they play their sixths and thirds and finally divide and echo the violins. Mendelssohn was a viola player himself and did much to restore the pride and self-confidence of that section of the orchestral strings. A good example of this is shown in the Introduction to the Scottish Symphony in which divided violas play a leading role.

Passing on to bar one-hundred-and-forty-four it is interesting to observe the enharmonic use of the F sharp of the D trumpets for G flat and the similar use of the F sharp timpano, showing Mendelssohn's acute alertness to the possibilities of limited means. Not many composers would have stopped to think whether a natural trumpet in D would be of any use in the key of B flat minor. The passage which starts at bar one-hundred-and-forty-nine is a notable example of climax-building, not by addition of fresh instruments (brass and drums are added as soon as the modulations permit) but by the use of dynamic markings applied to the full orchestra. The held notes on the oboes which

THE ELEMENTS OF ORCHESTRATION

easily penetrate the staccato of the rest of the instruments are a master-stroke. Their pungent tone gives an undoubted salty tang to the music. So we come to the peak of the climax at bar one-hundred-and-sixty-nine, but the tension and excitement is not immediately relaxed. The upward chromatic scale with brass and drums hammering away at their single notes tops the whole passage off magnificently. Forsyth in his *Orchestration* draws attention to the little run on the flutes at the end of this (bar one-hundred-and-seventy-eight or letter F) and likens it to " the little crest of spray flung into the air by the huge wave as it breaks ".

In his recapitulation, which begins at bar one-hundred-and-eighty, Mendelssohn is by no means content to repeat his ex-position, in fact he presents his material quite differently and much more briefly than he does in its first appearance. In bars one-hundred-and-eighty-six and one-hundred-and-eighty-seven, the clarinet is used in conjunction with horns and trumpets and balances very well with them. Probably it did so even better in Mendelssohn's time when the clarinet was more strident than it is today. The second subject is here given to clarinets (beginning at bar two-hundred-and-two with a very still and quiet string background). At bar two-hundred-and-seventeen *(Animato)* the coda begins and in it there is much brilliant writing for the violins. At bar two-hundred-and-thirty the second violins are written above the firsts for ten bars so as to get the maximum dash and accuracy for the semiquaver passages by giving them to the leading players. At bar two-hundred-and-forty-four (letter H) the 'cellos and basses are given a simplified form of the passage played by the upper strings, and the orchestra for several bars is divided into two parts, strings playing one line in three octaves and wind the other, also in three octaves. An original and tell-ing stroke is the *pp* octave F sharp at bar two-hundred-and-sixty-two held for four bars while the rest of the orchestra continues to play *ff*. This is taken over by the oboes so as not to overpower the flute and clarinet in bar two-hundred-and-sixty-six.

This score provides a remarkable example of imaginative genius combined with craftsmanship of the highest order. Closer study will reveal further felicitous technical details and cannot fail to instruct and stimulate the would-be orchestral composer or orchestrator, however far removed the idiom in which he is working may be from that of Mendelssohn. The principles we formulated after going through the Mozart movement are all endorsed here though the years which separated these two works had naturally brought changes of degree but not of kind, and in this overture the programmatic idea behind the music of course calls for a greater emphasis on colouristic technique than a purely symphonic work demands. Like all good programme music, however, *Fingal's Cave* is perfectly satisfactory apart from any extra-musical significance or inspiration because it is evocative rather than descriptive and exists in its own right without the need for any explanation apart from its title.

CHAPTER VII

IF WE add to the orchestra used by Mendelssohn in *Fingal's Cave* the following instruments, namely another pair of horns, three trombones and possibly one or two percussion players, we have the normal classical Full Orchestra. Later on the tuba was so often used that it could almost be regarded as a regular member of the brass section and large operatic and symphonic orchestras from the mid-nineteenth century onwards contained triple wood-wind, the third players often being called upon to play the " extra " instrument of each group. In large orchestras like this a third trumpet is also likely to be found, also a harp (sometimes two) and several percussion players.

No " rules " can be given for writing *tutti* passages. Much depends on the nature of the music itself, but certain physical facts are inescapable such as the dominance of the brass section over both strings and woodwind and the relative strength or weakness of instruments at certain pitches. In any example of *tutti* there is bound to be a good deal of doubling in order to get the tonal perspective right. It will be helpful to study such passages taken from well-known works chosen to show some of the ways in which composers have achieved clear, sonorous and well balanced effects when using the full resources of the orchestra.

(1) MOZART : Overture—*The Magic Flute.*

The first three bars show how chords can be laid out. In the first chord the top note is entrusted to flutes and oboes in unison.

The clarinets have the inner parts and the bassoons the bass. The chord is therefore complete on the woodwind. The root and fifth of the chord are played by horns and trumpets, the third being given to the second trombone, while the other two trombones play the root (E flat) in octaves. The chord is thus made very full and complete on the brass. The first and second violins play together the notes E flat and G in double stopping. This gives great power and a kind of rough edge to the sound. There is no fifth of the chord on the strings; Mozart here adopts the convention, upon which we have remarked before, of doubling the 'cellos and basses with his violas instead of giving them the B flat between the two violin notes, but the fifth of the chord is very strong on the brass and is reinforced also by the first clarinet (harsher in tone then than now) so that its absence from the string section is not noticeable. In the second (C minor) chord the arrangement is rather different. The strings are placed at the top of the chord with the flutes, oboes and clarinets, giving freshness and brilliance to the sonority. Note the wide spacing between second and bass trombones in this and the next chord. The second horn helps to fill this gap in the second chord and both horns do so in the third. Mozart was using an alto trombone and his first trombone part is therefore on the high side. It should be noted that the first trombone plays the top notes of the chords in the lower octave; in fact, if these chords were played by the trombones alone all the essentials would be there. In the third chord it will be noted that though it is a first inversion of the chord of E flat the third, G, is given to the second violins. This is somewhat unusual, the reason probably being that Mozart wanted the E flat and, as a string player, did not relish writing the fifth E flat and B flat as a double stop and so decided on this arrangement because he wished to use the E string on the second violins for the sake of brilliance.

(2)   BEETHOVEN. Symphony No. 5 in C minor.

The first twenty-two bars of the Finale provide our next example.

Beethoven brings in fresh instruments here; the piccolo, double bassoon and three trombones add severally height and brilliance,

strength and additional depth to the bass and tremendous power
to the whole structure. The violins in the first five bars play four
and three-part chords while the violas are placed low down in
their compass playing double-stops (except in the fourth bar
where they have to divide) and using tremolando bowing. In the
third bar the violas are the only instruments which sound continuously without quaver rests. 'Cellos and basses perform their
normal function of playing the bass together, but note the use of
the open 'cello C which with the open C of the violas lends a
decidedly rich sonority to the string tone. There is indeed a number of open strings employed in the violins also. This gives great
resonance and force to the string writing. Turning to the woodwind we find this section deployed over a wide compass. Flutes
and piccolo occupy the top octave, oboes and clarinets double
them at the octave below. Note that the first oboe and first
clarinet and the second oboe and second clarinet double one another, a much better procedure than giving the upper note to the
two oboes in unison and the lower to the two clarinets. Then
there is a gap of two octaves between these instruments and the
bassoons and well below them the double bassoon (sounding, we
remember, an octave lower than the written notes) plays the bass
part at sixteen-foot pitch. The bassoon writing here looks to the
eye a little thick, but combined with the violas it is adding
a warmth and richness to the lower reaches of the texture. Compared with the total sound of the rest of the orchestra these instruments are not obtrusive and can fill in the harmony at this
rather low pitch without the thickness of effect that would result
from more powerful combinations of instruments.

Beethoven's first six bars of melody can be played on the
natural horns and trumpets so that for once he is able to indulge
in the luxury of giving the tune to the brass as he does with the
big tune in the finale of the ninth at much greater length than
he is able to do here.

The trombones double the horns in unison, except in the first
chord of all, where they are up with the trumpets. This unison of
horns and trombones goes into the gap between the oboes and
clarinets and the bassoons. The trumpets double the oboes and
clarinets. A point worth noting in the third bar is the note F on
the second trombone on the second and fourth beats. This note

is unobtainable on the natural horn and therefore there is a momentary cessation of doubling between second horn and trombone so that the seventh of the chord, which otherwise only appears as part of the violin chords, can be powerfully sounded. The bass trombone naturally has the bass part of the structure and as this consists of tonic and dominant the timpani can be used without any inhibitions. Where the quaver scale passages come, starting at the sixth bar, the horns and trumpets have to be content to hammer out a simplified version of their rhythm on the monotone C. The piccolo helps a good deal here in bringing the top line into prominence, although this would be sufficiently prominent but not nearly so brilliant without it. Two oboes and clarinets add a great deal of volume to the first violins. Note that in bar eight Beethoven does not ask the bass trombone to play the four-quaver motif in the bass. The trombone trio always makes satisfactory three-part harmony and greatly helps in stabilising and strengthening the harmonic background. From bar thirteen onwards we find examples of something which is very commonly met with in orchestral writing, namely the clash of accented passing notes with their adjacent harmony notes on instruments of a different family. The Es and Ds and Cs resolving respectively on D, C and B are heard against these latter notes on horns, trumpets and trombones without any ambiguity of effect being felt by the listener. Beginners often write clumsy parts for instruments because of a fear of such clashes, and the result is far less clear than if the clashes were boldly written and the harmonic basis made plain to the listener's ear.

(3) WAGNER. Overture *Die Meistersinger,* bars 59 to 88.

We now take a big step forward in time and find fully chromatic writing for all four horns and two out of the three trumpets. In this particular extract not very much use is made of the third trumpet in C, which Wagner treats as a " natural " trumpet. The piccolo too is sparingly used in this passage. The nature of the tuba is fully understood by Wagner, who uses it as an independent instrument and not as a mere adjunct to the trombones.

Although we are using this as an example of *tutti,* all the instruments do not play incessantly but the effect is one of full orchestral writing and the rests which occur in the brass section serve to increase the point of the linear structure of the passage, for here the texture is contrapuntal and there is no mere filling in of the harmony anywhere.

The passage shows how four-part writing can be evenly distributed throughout the orchestra and a good balance achieved at a general level of *fortissimo*.

The top line is given to all the violins in unison at a very telling range. Next below (alto line) come the oboes and clarinets in unison doubled at the octave below by the third and fourth horns. At bar sixty the important note C sharp is reinforced by the second trombone marked *f* not *ff*. The tenor line is given to the powerful and sonorous combination of violas, 'cellos and first and second horn. At bar sixty-two Wagner solves a little problem very neatly. The tune really rises to high G at bar sixty-three, but the violins could not carry it on at such a high pitch, so oboes and clarinets are taken off the alto part in order, with the flutes added, to continue the quaver figure where the violins leave off. The trumpets (marked *forte*) take over from the oboes and clarinets and are given the notes which they and their attendant pair of horns would have if they had not been needed elsewhere. The violins are thus able, without any awkward leap, to resume their melody at the pitch at which they started it. The tenor trombones help to stabilise the texture and the bass of the structure is in the safe keeping of bassoons, tuba and double basses, while the bass trombone keeps silence. His tone would have been too brassy and obtrusive to blend in with the general smooth, though powerful, sonority.

At bar sixty-seven greater intensity is obtained by changes in the distribution of the parts. Piccolo, flutes, oboes, clarinets and first trumpet replace the violins on the top line while the first violins join the violas on what we have called the tenor line but which is now played by an octave-combination instead of being in unison as before. The third and fourth horns reinforce the 'cellos on the lower octave of the tenor line, and second trumpet, with some help from first and second horns, doubles the second violins at the octave below on the alto line. The bass part continues on the same instruments as before, but is joined at bar seventy-one by the bass trombone; the tuba at this point takes the sub-octave with the double basses instead of playing at the eight-foot pitch as heretofore.

At bar seventy-one also the second violins take over from the first trumpet and support the woodwind on the main tune, while the trumpets revert to a subsidiary role. The trombones here assume their normal procedure as a harmonic unit, supplying the majestic sequence of chords on which the passage is built.

At bar seventy-six the music for four bars becomes less contrapuntal in texture. The harp is added here but does not make its presence felt to any very appreciable extent though it does give a just perceptible stress to the weak beats.

Bar eighty sees the contrapuntal texture in evidence again. Note the telling unison of high violas and oboes supporting the first violins, with two bassoons, two horns and a trombone at the octave below making a double octave combination.

The main theme comes through well in spite of the height of the first violins against it. The piccolo, flutes, clarinets and third horn form a very powerful reinforcement to the second violins. The trumpets doubled at the lower octave by fourth horn and second trombone (the fourth horn joins in this part at bar eighty-one) take care of the third, or " tenor ", line and the double basses have at the octave above a unison of bass trombone and tuba. A dominant pedal-note on G is supplied, with unusual but very appropriate effect by the timpani only. The third trumpet makes brief appearances, its most effective use being made in bars eighty-seven and eighty-eight where it plays the opening notes of the theme. But attention here is forced on to the chromatic thirds, played in unison on first and second trumpets doubled by tenor trombones and violas and 'cellos. The 'cellos are often, as they are here, placed above the violas. This greatly increases the intensity and richness of the sound. Near the end of the overture the passage from bars one-hundred-and-eighty-eight to two-hundred-and-two provides a fine example of the use of active string figuration to add brilliance, life and vigour to the solid choral progressions of wind and brass. In two much earlier overtures, *Rienzi* and *Tannhäuser,* Wagner uses this idea but in a rather different way. In *Rienzi* the violins and violas play ascending flourishes during the fortissimo statement of the theme of the slow introduction. These are effective enough but have no thematic significance. Similarly in the famous trombone passage in *Tannhäuser* the violins decorate the score with scintillating downward scales in time with the triplet rhythm of the accompaniment, again having no thematic function. But in our *Meistersinger* example the first violins and violas reinforce the tune itself with brilliant flourishes while the second violins, 'cellos and basses develop previously heard figuration. The string writing here is therefore functional as well as decorative. From bar two-hundred-and-three to the end the music becomes solidly harmonic apart from the triplets which embellish the bass in the first four bars of this passage. It is instructive to notice here and elsewhere the rests in the brass parts. There is no very noticeable diminution in tone anywhere (though from a scientific point of view there must be) but the entries and brief exits of these powerful instruments invest what they have to say with far greater significance than if they were all playing all the time. From bar two-hundred-and-ten to the end everybody does play. Counterpoint is discarded and a magnificently solid coda finishes the overture. In studying the scores of Elgar, who learned much from Wagner's works, one is also struck by the confidence with which rests are written for instruments during passages which are essentially *tutti*. From a severely practical point of view this procedure has value in providing breathing spaces for the players of instruments whose continued use might be too fatiguing.

(4) Smetana. Overture, *The Bartered Bride*.

This opera was first performed in 1866, four years after the production of *Die Meistersinger* and it is interesting to compare the brass writing of the two composers in their overtures. One sees at once that Smetana, in spite of the brilliance and originality of his genius, was more conservative in his attitude to the horns and trumpets than Wagner. For, though there is evidence from the presence of some notes outside the harmonic series (and difficult to obtain by hand-stopping) that he was writing for players of valve-instruments, habit was too strong for him, and he mostly clung to the old "natural" horn and trumpet formulae, feeling safer with open notes and perhaps like Brahms, preferring their sound. If we look at the third and fourth horn parts in bars one-hundred-and-forty-four to one-hundred-and-sixty we find several Bs, As and Fs (on the bottom space) which are of course outside the natural series, and the first and second horns also have similar notes. Yet the general run of the parts is in accordance with the old pre-valve patterns. Still more is this true of the trumpet parts, which are confined to the natural notes practically all the time, though between bars four-hundred-and-twenty-two and four-hundred-and-forty there are a low D, a low F and a low F sharp, showing that Smetana envisaged the use of valve-trumpets. There is, however, nothing archaic about the sound of his orchestra. Let us look at the *tutti* starting at bar two-hundred-and-eighty-seven. This is based on strong diatonic harmony which favours the use of natural brass. Note the use of one pair of horns in F, the other in C, giving greater choice of open notes. The lay-out of this passage is simple and brilliantly effective. The thirds of the violins are reinforced by the upper woodwind, including piccolo at the octave above, the middle register of the orchestra being well filled by the brass. The 'cellos are divided into two parts, the first independent, the second playing with the basses. On looking back nearer the beginning of the overture we find the original reason for this division. At bar fifty-two Smetana doubles the entry of the violas with the 'cellos in unison to give greater attack and also perhaps because he did not trust the orchestral violists of his day to come in with sufficient confidence and authority. At bar seventy-three he is obliged to drop out the second half of the 'cellos in order to give support to the entry of the basses. In actual fact the best place to drop the second 'cellos would be at the *p subito* at bar fifty-seven. Having divided the 'cellos there he evidently decided that it would be agreeable to keep them so for much of the time, both to help the violas in further running passages and to enrich the string harmony. In the passage we are studying, violas and first 'cellos carry on the quaver figuration from the previous section for eight bars, thus neatly dovetailing things together and keeping up the feeling of busy-ness. The layout of the brass harmony is admirably full. If difficulty is found with mental transposition the chords should be written out in their actual sounds, remembering that first and second horns and trumpets are in F and third and fourth horns are in C. At bar three-hundred-and-five all quaver movement stops, first 'cellos join seconds and basses, and the whole orchestra hammers out the same rhythm. Note the way the trumpets reinforce the climactic notes of each two-bar phrase and the distribution of the harmony in the woodwind section. Close harmony like this in the top register of the orchestra adds greatly to the brilliance of a chordal passage of this kind. At bars two-hundred-and-thirty and two-hundred-and-thirty-two the timpani have neither the bass nor the root of the chord but the seventh because that is the only harmony note available. The effect is perfectly satisfactory. The trombone chords are excellently placed for a crackling attack. Note the bold way in which the bass trombone jostles his way through his colleagues at bar three-hundred-and-fifteen. In this same bar the flutes are lifted up to the high octave because the piccolo part is getting too low for effectiveness and is jettisoned in the next bar.

(5) BRAHMS. Symphony No. 4 in E minor.

We here find the composer taking a leaf out of Beethoven's book and saving up his trombones for the last movement to which, at the very outset, they lend impressive weight and colour. Brahms's scoring has often been criticised for turgidity and dullness, but actually he used the orchestra in his own individual way, in accord with the character of his music, and the sort of brilliance we associate with, say, Rimsky-Korsakov's scores would have been out of place. He did, however, inhibit himself by the somewhat archaic attitude which he adopted towards the horns and trumpets, forcing himself to use open notes wherever possible. This may have resulted in some advantage in the matter of purity and fullness of tone but when we compare his orchestral sound with that of some of his juniors and contemporaries, Wagner for instance, his methods seem reactionary and hidebound by tradition as regards the mechanics of orchestration. Near the beginning of this movement (the Finale) we find at bar twenty-five a short *tutti*, marked *f*, not *ff*, in which the woodwind are the protagonists and are clearly audible although all the rest of the orchestra is playing. The strings have big pizzicato chords, easy to play and therefore likely to sound confident and well in tune. The top line of the first violin part picks out the notes of the passacaglia theme which is decorated with passing notes in the woodwind. One pair of horns, first trumpet and first trombone back this up. The woodwind are laid out in a particularly Brahmsian way, though this way of using them had been demonstrated by the classical masters long before his time. Thirds and sixths used in double and triple octaves are powerful, and when marked *f ben marc*, which is equivalent to *ff*, come through the mainly detached chords of the strings and brass. That is the real point. If sustained harmony had been used the woodwind would have practically disappeared, and if the principal notes of their version of the theme had not been reinforced the musical sense of the passage would have been lost. It is interesting to observe Brahms's use of the double bassoon here. It plays the whole of the bass part which is otherwise split up between 'cellos plus string basses and the bass trombone. The double bassoon has considerable power and its ability to add weight to the sixteen-foot tone of the orchestra is very useful. Note that the pair of horns in E are kept to open notes (except for one E flat). The other pair in C here have a rather unusual number of stopped notes for Brahms. Later on in the same movement, at bar one-hundred-and-ninety-three a more powerful climax is reached. Here all the instruments except the trombones are marked *ff*, the trombones have *f* in their parts, an adjustment which may well have been made at rehearsal. Brahms wished to avoid a blasting tone on these chords which would have competed too violently with the persistent Es on the horns and trumpets. This *tutti* is as simple in its layout as it is impressive and effective. Each department of the orchestra has its own individual contribution to make to the ensemble. The strings as usual have the most excitable rhythm in triplets, the woodwind in straight quavers and the brass and drums in crotchets. At bar two-hundred-and-one the counter melody given to the violins and violas in rapidly repeated bowing is doubled by oboes and bassoons and comes over clearly because the big chords on the rest of the woodwind and brass only appear on the second beat of each bar. The horns and trumpets are given triplet repetitions while the trombones have straight quavers, more in keeping with their dignified habits. The passacaglia theme is kept well to the fore as it is played by first flute in its top register, first clarinet and first trumpet at the octave below, and first horn and first trombone at the octave below that.

(6) DVORAK. Symphony No. 5 in E minor. *From the New World.*

Here we find Dvorak still using in 1893 horns and trumpets crooked in different keys, though he is freer than Brahms in his use of chromatic notes for these instruments.

The *tutti* which begins eight bars before No. 8 in the first movement shows several points of interest. First of all there is the treatment of the theme in the bass, allotted to bassoons, two trombones and 'cellos and basses. The high-placed chords on woodwind and tremolo strings, backed up by horns and trumpets below, can be played as loud as you like without any danger of swamping the trombones. The bass trombone is left out. The theme lies a little high for him at the pitch of the tenor trombones and would sound rather coarse an octave below. But probably the real reason for leaving him out is that he is needed to help the brasses at the fifth bar of the passage and might go on playing too loudly (his entry is marked *f*, not *ff*) if he had taken part in the preceding very prominent passage. The trumpets play their little thematic repetitions in a key which Brahms, with his predilections for open notes, would have viewed with distaste, much as he admired Dvorak's work. They are doubled by oboes —a favourite device of Tchaikovsky's, by the way. At No. 8 the passage is repeated a semitone higher with the same scoring except that the timpani's notes are now available and so a good deal of extra force can be added to the music. At the ninth bar after No. 8, we have another example of the use of detached chords which enable the violin figures to stand out clearly without having to be doubled by woodwind. The doubling by flutes in the first four bars does not make any appreciable difference to the strength of the violins. It is interesting to note that Dvorak uses in this passage (ninth bar of No. 8) the same method of using the violins as we found at the beginning of the Finale of Beethoven's C minor Symphony, leaving a big gap between violins and violas (which is, of course, filled by wind instru-

108 THE ELEMENTS OF ORCHESTRATION

ments) and providing a little extra feeling of excitement both
from the sound and sight of the violas fiddling away for dear life.
The passage immediately following this *tutti*, where the oboes
have the theme is a good example of a way of using the trombones, with horns to fill in the extra notes required to provide a
quiet background to instruments which could never compete
with them in even an *mf* passage. Dvorak, by the way, uses the
alto clef for his tenor trombones, a hangover from the days of
the alto trombone.

We have omitted many famous composers and famous works
in our brief survey of the orchestral *tutti* in the nineteenth century, but the list would be too incomplete altogether if there were
no mention of Tchaikovsky whose scores provide so many examples of simple yet immensely effective writing. Rimsky-
Korsakov's book provides many examples of varied combinations
of instruments from his own works. It is therefore unnecessary to
do more than pay him a passing gesture of admiration and
respect and to refer the reader to his *Principes d'Orchestration*.
Tchaikovsy's last symphony (No. 6, *Pathétique*) can be regarded
as a kind of last will and testament of his methods of handling
the orchestra and indeed contains a great many interesting and
beautiful effects which must have seemed extremely novel when
they were first heard. Although it was written at the same time
(1893) as Dvorak's *New World* it shows a much more " modern "
attitude towards orchestration. Wagner of course shares this distinction with him and so does Richard Strauss, but both these
composers required a much larger orchestral apparatus in most of
their works than Tchaikovsky, who was usually content with
double woodwind, except for three flutes, the third alternating
with piccolo, two trumpets and the usual four horns, three trombones, tuba, timpani and modest demands in the way of percussion. He reserved the harp for use in the theatre or for dramatic works like the Overture-Fantasy *Romeo and Juliet* from which
examples have already been drawn in this book. His music is
highly emotional but is controlled by a truly musical mind and
we find in his works a very fine regard for the exact placing and
spacing of notes which show him to have been the possessor of
a polished and highly accomplished technique. Not for nothing
did he admire Mozart beyond all other composers.

His *tutti* are often based on warm lyrical melodies and he is fond of using the whole mass of strings except the double basses as a melodic unit playing in three octaves, the wind and brass supplying the harmony and contrapuntal interest, if any. Sometimes the 'cellos do not take part in the tune, the three octave combination being then simply laid out for first and second violins and violas, as at the *Andante*, fourteen bars after letter F in the First Movement of the *Pathétique*. Note the dynamic markings of the various departments of the orchestra and the way the trumpets and trombones are used against the strings in a very much more independent manner than in any of the *tutti* so far examined. The Russian composers seem to have settled for the standard valve-horn in F earlier than was done in other countries, and in this work Tchaikovsky uses trumpets in B flat and A rather than the old F and E instruments. At the eighth bar after Q in the same movement the composer wants the highest degree of expressive intensity and this he achieves by scoring his octave string combination for first and second violins in octaves, and dividing the violas in octaves so that one half plays in unison with the seconds and the other in the octave below. The first violins are doubled in unison by three flutes. The harmony is supplied by horns and trumpets aided by oboes and clarinets, the trombones and tuba play responsive phrases to the strings, while bassoons, timpani and double basses supply the F sharp pedal-bass.

Another arrangement of strings is to be found at letter E in the last movement. Here both second violins and violas are divided in octaves so as to give the following lay-out: top line first violins and half the seconds; middle line the lower half of the seconds and the top half of the violas; third line the lower half of the violas and the 'cellos. Harmony is provided by woodwind, and canonic imitation of the string melody is shared by trumpets and trombones for the one part and horns for the other, both groups playing in octaves. The division of the second violins ensures that the high notes given to the first violins do not sound thin and the high-lying first-viola part adds a good deal of intensity to the middle line of the triple octave combination because the violas are playing on their first string all the way through, or practically so. This is another good example of a passage in which each department of the orchestra is allotted a different task—chords repeated in triplet rhythm on the wind, counterpoint on the brass and principal melody on the strings. Bass trombone, tuba and double basses supply the bass quite sufficiently. Note at letter F the way the climactic top B of the strings is reinforced by the horns and also the way the triplet rhythm comes into its own at the same point, being hammered out by the heavy brass.

We might end this short survey of nineteenth century *tutti* writing, woefully incomplete thought it is, by attempting to orchestrate for full orchestra two different types of passages. The last few bars of Brahms's *Variations on a Hungarian Song* Op. 21, No. 2 will serve our purpose well for the first example. Here they are in their original version for piano:

Ex:36

As a discipline, and also in the interests of stylistic conformity, let us make the transcription in such a way as we think Brahms himself might have done, confining our horn and trumpet parts to the notes of the harmonic series, in other words writing for natural horns and trumpets. We will allow ourselves a piccolo and a double bassoon, and though Brahms did occasionally use the tuba we will dispense with it here.

In order to give ourselves a greater variety of available notes from the horn quartet we will write for one pair in G and the other in D. The trumpets will of course be in D. Needless to say if our transcription were performed today the horn parts would all be played on F horns and the trumpets on B flat instruments, the players transposing their parts with the ease born of practice and experience in playing classical works. Three timpani are at our disposal. This firmly diatonic passage can best be served by tuning the drums in G, A and D. Bass drum and cymbals could be used but we will resist the temptation as they might introduce a slightly vulgar taint out of keeping with our pious desire to save the composer from more revolutions in his grave than we can help.

This is not from its nature a passage in which the different departments of the orchestra can be employed on figuration of their own. A massive effect is the aim. We will decide on the following scheme:

In order to achieve the *marcato* effect indicated by the composer the strings can be given double and triple stops—the upper strings, that is—'cellos and basses will play the bass part in octaves, and we have to remember that bottom D is not available on the basses. We want a rhythmical attack from the strings and will write the chords for violins and violas as quavers separated by quaver rests. The 'cellos and basses will play crotchets as in the original. I think we will keep the thick chords in the bass on the last beat of bar three and the first of bar four. Brahms was fond of that kind of spacing, so we will retain it and give the low sixths D—B to 'cellos in double stopping, second bassoon and double bassoon.

Turning to the woodwind the piccolo will play the top line at its written pitch (sounding an octave higher) and the flutes will make three-part harmony with it except for any notes which are not high enough to be really telling on the piccolo. In such places the first flute will play in unison with the piccolo. In the last two bars a more brilliant finish would be obtained if the first violins carried their line up into the high octave. The piccolo can also do this effectively in the highest octave of the orchestra. Oboes and clarinets will be kept high with a big space between them and the bassoons. The second bassoon will play the bass line with the double bassoon at the octave lower. The first bassoon can be given a middle-register part, more for the purpose of giving him something that feels more important than just playing in unison with his partner than for any appreciable contribution to the powerful mass of sound we are producing.

Trumpets, horns and tenor trombones fill the gap left between the high woodwind and the bass most adequately. Apart from the high Bs in the second bar the first trumpet can play the tune doubled by the third horn (in D) at the lower octave. We will write the trumpet and horn parts first in order to exploit their limited range of notes to the full, and will then add the tenor trombones which will be able to supply notes which we need and which cannot be played as open notes by our natural horns and trumpets. The bass trombone will naturally play the bass line, but we will decide not to give him the quaver triplets because of the military band effect this would give. We shall be able to find notes for the timpani to play throughout if we remember that it is not essential to give them the bass of a chord so long as the note we do write is a factor in the harmony. It needs to be said that the chords as laid out for the piano will be filled in so that there are no great gaps between the bass and the next notes above it. In the third and fourth bars from the end, the D, which appears between the bass octaves, can be given to the timpani. It is not necessary to give it to any other instrument.

Having decided the plan of operations it now only remains to put it into musical notation. This is best done by dealing with each section of the orchestra separately. Different types of music may demand different orders of precedence, but in most instances either the strings or brass are laid out first. Of course an eye and ear on what the other sections are going to do have to be kept, and at first it may be difficult to carry details in one's head without writing them down, but it is no use writing each chord from top to bottom of the score. The essence of music is motion and that method is far too static and lifeless in its approach.

In the exercise we are now considering the music is so direct and simple in texture that, having decided on our general plan, we can start with the strings, then add the brass and finally the woodwind. The timpani part can be added last of all, or as an adjunct to the brass.

The double and triple stopping must be kept simple and easy. The key of D major abounds in easy chords for strings and there is almost bound to be a pretty liberal sprinkling of open strings. It does not matter if notes are reduplicated in the chords but we will try to make them as full as we can, ease of playing being the first consideration if we are to achieve the maximum of confidence in attack and accuracy of intonation.

With these considerations in view our string parts can be written as on page 114 (Ex. 37).

The full score has, we must imagine, been ruled out in the usual way with woodwind at the top, brass and timpani in the middle and strings at the bottom in the conventional order. The woodwind and brass staves are at present empty and await our attention. Let us now deal with the brass and timpani according to the plan described on page 111. (Ex. 38).

It now remains to fill in the woodwind staves. The piccolo is played by the third flute player and its part is therefore written on the second stave below the flutes in spite of being above them in pitch. Clarinets in A are chosen as this is a " sharp " key. The woodwind here fulfils its normal and proper function of reinforcing the upper partials of the brass and thus adds bite and sparkle to the orchestral sound. (Ex. 39, page 116.)

H

Example 37

Ex:38

Example 38

Example 39

Our full score is now complete. If the reader thinks it worth while he can copy out the above on score-paper of eighteen or twenty staves. It is always wise to leave an empty staff above the first violins and it makes a score easier to read if the bar lines are not drawn continuously down the page but are ruled with breaks between the sections of the orchestra.

I would like to emphasise that it is only in the elementary stages that a *tutti* has to be built up like this, section by section, but it is a good way for an inexperienced writer to work and teaches the importance of planning the general treatment and lay-out before getting down to detailed work.

The writing for natural horns and trumpets in the above exercise is deliberately archaic and is of course never done now nor indeed has it been the practice of most composers for over a century. But it does inculcate a sense of style in using these instruments just as the study of sixteenth-century counterpoint is beneficial to composers who will probably never want to write their own music in that style. It would of course be ridiculous to write original music today employing natural horns and trumpets, though this might well be done in transcribing old music for orchestra for the sake of preserving a sense of period and style.

Let us now rewrite the brass parts in our Brahms exercise using the standard F horns and B flat trumpets in use today. The tenor trombone parts will also be altered a little to fit in with the new horn and trumpet parts. In loud passages two horns in unison are pretty well equivalent to one trumpet or one trombone. It is common therefore to find the horn parts written in two parts, first and third horns on the upper notes and second and fourth on the lower. Rimsky-Korsakov seems to have been the first writer to draw attention to this acoustical fact and many examples of two-part writing for horns when filling in the harmony of trumpets and trombones are to be found in his scores. This method is also a feature of much of Tchaikovsky's *tutti* writing. Three-part writing for four horns is also not uncommon especially where it is desired to make one line specially prominent. It should not, therefore, be thought necessary always to use the horn quartet as a four-part combination. If this were done it would often result in undue thickness of brass harmony. In quiet passages four-part harmony is fascinating on the horns and of

course the rule that two horns equal one trumpet or one trombone does not apply in dynamics below *f* and *ff*. Where only two
horns are used it may sometimes be necessary to mark them one
degree higher dynamically than the trumpets and trombones, but
here again this would only be done in fairly loud passages. If the
horn parts in our following little exercise be carefully examined
some of these points will be observed. The string and woodwind
parts are imagined to be the same as before.

As we have remarked earlier in this book, composers vary in their habits regarding the use of key signatures for horns and trumpets. Some retain the old custom, derived from pre-valve days, of omitting key signatures and putting in the necessary accidentals. This has the advantage to the score-reader and conductor of guiding the eye to these parts and thus orientating the position of other neighbouring instruments in a crowded score. The provision of key signatures gives the players a greater sense of tonality of course, and is some safeguard to those composers who are inclined to be forgetful of their accidentals. It is not a matter of great importance which method is adopted, and there is no really valid reason why players of these instruments should not be as much at home in all reasonable keys as pianists or string players or anybody else. Habit is very strong, however, and the signatures of five or six sharps and flats do not " look right " to those who have spent their lives among scores most of which dispense with all key signatures for horns and trumpets.

It will be noticed that in both brass-section versions I have not given the bass trombone the drop onto the low D in Brahms's original left-hand part in bars two, four and nine. The tone is rather coarse down there and bassoons, double bassoons and 'cellos can have the octave drop though the basses cannot. So as it would also involve a big change of position I thought it best to repeat the D where it stands.

Our next exercise is taken from Elgar's Organ Sonata in G (part of the Coda of the last movement). (Ex. 41.)

This passage, in fact the whole sonata, is very orchestral in style although it is extremely effective on the organ. The work was written in 1895, four years before the *Enigma* Variations. It would therefore seem suitable to use the same-sized orchestra as Elgar did in that work rather than the larger Wagnerian forces employed in his later symphonic and choral works. Double woodwind (second flute doubling piccolo) with the addition of a double bassoon; four horns, three trumpets, three trombones and tuba; timpani, two percussion players, or better three, as Elgar expects the second player to play bass drum and cymbals together—a possible procedure if one cymbal is attached to the bass drum, but not very satisfactory—and strings. Elgar also writes an ad lib. organ part, but we will not follow his example there. It would

Example 41

Ex. 41 (Continued)

be redundant to use an organ in a transcription of an organ work.

We will begin by making a general reconnaissance of the extract and plan out, as we did in the Brahms exercise, the broad outlines of a scheme. We are justified in using our full resources as the composer gives the indication " Full Organ " nineteen bars before. In the first four bars the main thematic interest is in the bass and it would be good to throw all our reserves of bass instruments into it, including all the trombones with tuba at the sub-octave. On the bass, then, we will have the two bassoons and double bassoon, trombones and tuba and 'cellos and basses. The first chord will be played by the whole of the rest of the orchestra, the second beat chord of the dominant seventh could be given to the three trumpets with two horns in unison supplying the bottom note of it. The strings and high woodwind would then enter on the top E with great effect, trumpets and horns still supporting them. The little semiquaver run in bars three and four would go well on violas and clarinets doubled by the horns. As it is a very rapid passage for horns it might be safer to give the first seven notes of it to the first and third horns in unison and the remaining notes to the second and fourth. These latter would come in on the note (F sharp) on which the first pair leave off so as to ensure smoothness. At this speed it will be advisable to slur the clarinets and horns, but the violas can use a separate bow for each note. We will, by the way, use a piccolo instead of second flute throughout. Starting at bar five and for the next four bars the top line will be played by the first violins, flute and piccolo. It could be doubled at the lower octave also, and for this we could use second violins, violas and clarinets. In order to get approximately equal strength on each of these two lines the second violins could be divided, playing in octaves, so that the top line is further strengthened by half the second violins whilst the other half doubles the violas and clarinets in unison. In bars five and six the left-hand part can be played by 'cellos and all four horns in unison. On the second beat of bar six these will separate out, the four horns playing the G and B flat, and the 'cellos the E in preparation for their descent in the next two bars (pedal part). The oboes and two trumpets can play the inner parts given to the R.H. in these same bars (five and six) and in bars seven and eight flute and oboes can play the staccato chords, omitting the semiquavers, doubled below by the three trumpets doing the same thing. In bar eight the bass could be doubled at the octave higher, coming in on the quaver E before the bar-line. The tenor trombones could do this, also the 'cellos, the basses coming in at this same point, taking over from the 'cellos and strengthened by the tuba. The bass trombone will have the pedal part of bars seven and eight as it stands, so will the bassoons. The double bassoon will enter with the tuba and double basses. Bars nine to twelve we will leave for further consideration after we have thought about what follows them. Bars thirteen to eighteen can best be done by giving the top line to the strings in octaves (first and second violins on top, violas and 'cellos below. The 'cellos' part can be eased by dropping a fourth on to the crotchets on the second beats instead of rising a fifth from bar fifteen onwards). The harmony will be given to horns, trumpets, oboes and bassoons. The tenor trombones will rest through these bars so as to come in with fresh vigour at bar nineteen with the L.H. part. The sustained G minims can be given to the horns with the addition of the octave above, two horns to each note. The trumpets can double the trombones at the octave above, two on the top line and one in unison with the first trombone. The bass trombone is required to give its weight to the pedal D from bars thirteen to eighteen and to the rhythmical pedal G from bar nineteen to the end. The R.H. figures in sixths can be given to the strings (violas and 'cellos below with 'cellos above violas) and woodwind, the piccolo and flute an octave above the violins, the oboes in unison with them and the clarinets with the violas and 'cellos. In view of the pedal part in bars twenty-three, twenty-four and twenty-five it may be advisable to keep the bass at the written pitch, only using the sub-octave in the last three bars, but that can be settled when we come actually to put the notes into the score.

In the final variation of the *Enigma*, Elgar uses mainly side drum (one player) and bass drum and cymbals (possible, as we have pointed out, for one player). This will do well here too. Alternate rolls on timpani and side drum will help the effect of the octave leaps in the bass in bars twenty-three, twenty-four and twenty-five. Elgar puts in a short sharp jab on the upper pedal G in the very last bar of all. This could be given to the percussion, with a whack also on the timpani at the end of his roll on G.

With regard to the tuning of the timpani; of course we need G and D, and for this passage we will assume that there has been time to retune the top drum to E flat for the bass. I use the word " retune " deliberately because it is very unlikely that E flat would be useful throughout the movement. G, C, and D would probably be the most likely notes for the general run of the movement though there would no doubt be changes of tuning from time to time.

We will now go back to bars nine to twelve which need careful consideration. Those who have read my book *Orchestral Technique* (O.U.P.) will realise that it is not always possible to be literal in one's translation from one medium to another. This rapid flourish on the full organ is effective enough on that instrument but would be unorchestral in style if put on to the orchestra as it stands because it is so obviously based on keyboard technique and is unidiomatic for strings and brass. We can and will distribute the arpeggio in its original form between the woodwind instruments but the strings must have some other version of it. My solution, which is offered with some diffidence, is to give the strings in octaves a telescoped arrangement of the arpeggio, the semiquaver movement being supplied by double bowing of each note. Meanwhile the brass hold the chord, attacking it pianissimo and swelling up to fortissimo. The pedal E flat has the double basses, double bassoon, two horns, tuba, bass trombone and timpani to give it substance; this ought to be enough.

I have set out this passage in full score instead of in sections as was done with the Brahms exercise.

The writing of the three trumpet parts on one staff is done to save space, but might cause complications if their parts were more rhythmically independent of each other than they are here.

One point calls for comment in the writing for double basses from bar nine to bar eighteen. Repeated or syncopated short notes are used for these long pedal notes. This is not noticed by the listener as other powerful instruments are sustaining the same note, but it means that the double basses are producing more tone and making a more valuable contribution than they would if they were given the long sustained notes as they stand in the original. For the same reason the 'cellos are given the E flat in bars nine to twelve as repeated semiquavers. This also backs up the rapid bowing of the upper string parts. I have written for the double bassoon as an " ad lib." instrument. It is always wiser to do this as players of this instrument are not always easily found and every " extra " means more expense. At the same time it is a very nice instrument to have in an orchestra if circumstances allow as it gives strength where it is perhaps most needed in the lowest depths and can get quite a number of notes below the reach of the double basses and tuba.

Example 42

CHAPTER VIII

SOME ASPECTS OF ORCHESTRATION IN THE
TWENTIETH CENTURY

DURING THE thirty years or so which separated the death of
Wagner and the beginning of the 1914-18 war composers were
attracted by the almost limitless opportunities offered by the use
of very large orchestras, and the greatness of a work was
measured to some extent by the length of time it occupied in performance and the number of performers it employed. The rich
and luscious sounds produced by large masses of instruments
suited very well the ideas and aspirations of the late romantics
and the harsh realities of economic necessity had not yet inter-
posed financial barriers between composers and the realisation of
their sometimes rather extravagant dreams. Richard Strauss's
earlier symphonic poems did not require more than the normal
Wagnerian orchestra based upon triple woodwind, but in the
last years of the nineteenth century we find him demanding
quadruple woodwind, eight horns, five trumpets and so on in
Heldenleben and in works like the *Sinfonio Domestica* and
Alpine Symphony he also wrote for vast orchestras. Bruckner had
already availed himself of " Wagner Tubas " and Mahler employed large forces in his symphonic works, including solo voices
and chorus. Scriabin, in works like *Prometheus* and *The Poem of
Ecstasy*, also wrote for a very large orchestra and Stravinsky's
three famous ballets, particularly *The Rite of Spring*, made big
demands. In our own country Elgar did not make use of outsize
orchestras in his symphonies or in *Falstaff*. He was content with
triple woodwind and normal brass, though he did introduce a
fourth member into the clarinet group in the shape of the E flat

instrument in his symphonies. Vaughan Williams also confined himself to the Wagnerian orchestra in his *London Symphony* but used two cornets as well as two trumpets. Holst in *The Planets* wrote for quadruple woodwind, using all the " extras ", including alto flute and bass oboe (heckelphone). He also wrote for six horns, four trumpets and tenor and bass tuba. Instances of the use of large orchestras during this period are too numerous to need further mention in detail, but it must be remarked that the skill of orchestral performers had kept pace with the demands of the most exacting composers as it still does. Sibelius, who wrote four of his symphonies before 1914, was content with the Tchaikovsky symphony orchestra, though he did favour the use of a third trumpet.

Since in large orchestras an increase in numbers in one department is matched by a corresponding increase in the others the relative strength of the sections remains much the same as it did in the mid-nineteenth century and although composers varied enormously in their acceptance and exploitation of the new harmonic freedom which had become available to them and although music was becoming more complex in texture the layout of the *tutti* was still governed by the same natural laws of balance as before. Mutes were, however, frequently (too frequently perhaps) applied to the brass which reduced their tonal volume, but the special menacing and dramatic effect obtained when muted brass is blown loudly became a prominent feature of the scores of some composers of that time to an irritating extent. No really new tone-colours were added to those already present, but fresh tints and shades were lent to them by the use of the rarer members of the various woodwind families, and by the exploration of unusual combinations of instruments. Not only the skill but the musicianship of orchestral players became sharpened to the importance of realising subtle effects of phrasing, tone and nuance. Those were the days when composers really had new worlds to conquer but when those who were content to produce works of originality and vitality from traditional material were welcome too, so that works like Elgar's *Falstaff* and Stravinsky's *The Rite of Spring* were able peacefully to co-exist after the first brief clamour against the latter work had died down. When we consider that the pre-1914 era also contained

I

130   THE ELEMENTS OF ORCHESTRATION

practically all Debussy's output and much of Ravel's as well as the early but challenging works of Schönberg, Webern and Berg we may well marvel at the fecundity of musical invention which was released in those years. Schönberg, by the way, used colossal forces in his *Gurrelieder* and his *Five Orchestral Pieces* were very fully scored in their original version which contained the rare contrabass clarinet, even now, alas, almost exclusively confined to large American wind bands.

After the 1914-1918 war most of the world was too impoverished to be able to afford to support very large orchestras and composers realised that they would have to be content with relatively modest resources. This chimed in with the general change of musical climate away from the romantic and the colossal. It is customary now to denigrate the 'twenties which those who lived through them did not realise were " silly ". The anti-romantic attitude was certainly exaggerated as all anti-movements are bound to be, but some good works were written and experiments were made in the use of unusually constituted orchestras and chamber-music combinations. The twenties also saw the invention and application of serial composition and twelve-note music which were destined to claim much attention in the late fifties and early sixties. In this country such works as Vaughan Williams's *Pastoral Symphony,* Bliss's *Colour Symphony,* Holst's *Hymn of Jesus,* Lambert's *Rio Grande* and Walton's *Façade* are still firmly established in the regular repertoire, and though the last two works named are gay and amusing none of them can be called exactly " silly ".

Stravinsky in his *L'histoire du Soldat* used a small miscellaneous collection of instruments in virtuoso fashion, influenced by jazz. He also wrote for wind alone *(Symphonies of Wind Instruments)* and strings alone *(Apollon Musagete),* for wind and double-basses (Piano concerto), for large orchestras without violins and violas *(Symphonies des Psaumes)* and so on, showing that composers were not obliged to accept the conventional orchestral ensemble if it did not suit their purposes. Lambert's *Rio Grande* mentioned above is scored for strings, brass, percussion and piano. The years between the wars were not without works written for large forces, e.g. Walton's *Belshazzar's Feast.* (But his First Symphony is scored for the normal Tchaikovsky orchestra.) Bartok explored fascinating sonorities both in works employing the conventional orchestra and in such pieces as *Music for Strings, Percussion and Celesta* and *Sonata for two pianos and percussion*. Mention of pianos and percussion calls to mind Stravinsky's *Les Noces* written as a ballet and scored for voices, four pianos and percussion. Hindemith has on the whole used a fairly large normal symphony orchestra, but in 1931 he wrote *Konzertmusik* for piano, brass and harps, and his concerto for organ and chamber orchestra explores unfamiliar sonorities.

Since the second world war orchestras (in this country at any rate) have had difficulty in keeping going and most have only managed to do so with the help of the Arts Council and municipal grants. Musicians now are quite rightly paid much higher rates than they used to receive and demands for extra players are not very popular with concert promoters, especially when they come from relatively unknown composers with little box-office appeal. It is therefore more advisable than ever to be economical in the use of instruments and to keep their numbers down to the minimum possible for the artistic presentation of the composer's imaginings. Works are of course written for, and are played by, symphony orchestras of normal size, but the days of mammoth combinations are over. Earlier in this book I mentioned Britten's use of a small chamber orchestra of expert players for many of his operas and his skilful employment of alternative instruments by his solo woodwind group. Instrumental colour has now become an integral part of the composer's basic ideas and the tendency to use the pure sounds of individual instruments rather than blending them by unison doubling encourages the use of small bodies of players. When a full orchestra is used it is quite possible that it will never be employed in *tutti* at all, but will be treated as a reservoir from which contrasted groups of instruments can be drawn. A good example of this is to be found in Stravinsky's *Agon,* and Britten in his orchestral music, though not eschewing *tutti* altogether, is also fond of this sectional method of scoring.

There is so much going on in music today that it is not possible to suggest to the serious student whose ambitions lie in the direction of composition that he can do more than keep in touch with what is new and choose or hew out for himself a technical method which seems most adequate to what he wants to say. There are still composers, perhaps the most important are Britten and Shostakovitch, whose music is based on tonality and as Schönberg said years ago there is still something new to be said in C major by anyone sufficiently inventive to discover it.

Meanwhile the budding composer will be well advised to grasp any opportunity that may offer itself (and indeed to create such opportunities for himself) of writing and arranging music for his local amateur orchestral society or school orchestra making use, as Bach and other illustrious predecessors did, of local resources. In the next two chapters I shall attempt to give some practical advice about cueing down for small and incomplete orchestras music originally written for normal (but of course not enormous) combinations.

CHAPTER IX

CUEING MISSING PARTS

IN RECENT years there has been a large increase in the number of boys and girls learning wind instruments at school. Fairly satisfactory results can be obtained much more quickly on these instruments than on strings and learning " music " has ceased to be looked upon as necessarily synonymous with struggling with the piano. Consequently most schools of any size possess some sort of orchestra, some well balanced and complete, others consisting of a collection of enthusiastic young people eager to make music together and to try their hand at some of the easier classics. When they leave school they probably wish to continue playing in orchestras and join the local amateur orchestral society. The trouble is that the constitution of such orchestras is often unconventional, to say the least, though schools try to steer their pupils towards learning instruments that are likely to be wanted in the orchestra in the foreseeable future.

Many publishers issue music specially written or arranged for school orchestras in which cueing has been carefully and ingeniously carried out. But it is not always possible to cater for particular orchestras by supplying ready-made material. One school or amateur orchestra may possess a very competent first clarinet, a good bassoon, two or three beginners on the oboe, no flute and no violas, so that to get the best results the ability of the players has to be taken into account as well as the holes in the ensemble. If the orchestra is very heterogeneous and unbalanced a competent pianist can be a great help in holding it together. Piano conductor parts are usually supplied containing all important cues but it is of course better to do without the support of the piano. Third violin parts in lieu of violas can also be useful.

133

Let us take some odd combinations of instruments at random and see what we can do with them. Only simple music will be used as our players are none of them anywhere near professional standard.

Our first example is an orchestra consisting of one flute (not bad but rather timid at present) one oboe (very keen and improving rapidly—tone not very well controlled yet, inclined to be too penetrating), five clarinets (one quite good and reliable, two fairly good on simple parts which do not go at all high), two trumpets (good), one trombone (rather a beginner), timpani and percussion (several players of various instruments if required) no violas but fairly numerous violins.

We are fortunate in having two members of the staff among the violins and another plays the double bass. There are two 'cellos, one a promising boy and the other one of the parents who lives close by and enjoys lending a hand—quite good too but not a very good sight-reader, especially in the tenor clef.

Let us see what can be done with the second movement (allegretto) of Haydn's *Military* Symphony, No. 11 in G major.

We have chosen this partly because it gives our percussion something to do. There is not anything for them, except the timpani, in the rest of the programme planned for the next concert, and we want them to have a look in somewhere.

It is rather unfortunate that we have no bassoon. He is in quarantine for the rest of the term and so will not be available for the concert.

The first thing that strikes our eye is the important part for violas. They are divided in places and have an unwontedly independent part for Haydn. We have eight violins, and cannot very well allot more than two to the viola part. Our two members of staff cannot be spared because they are needed as leaders of the first and second violins respectively so two of the boys will have to play third violin. Smith and Jones are fairly confident players and are sensible enough to enjoy playing independent parts. They must be made to feel it is a compliment to be asked to play third violin, as indeed it is.

Our only bass wind instrument is the trombone and he must be given an easy part.

Here are the first four bars in their original form :

Ex: 43

So far so good. Our timid flautist is given a good start playing in unison with the first violins, and can warm up on that. He has a wholesome fear of playing out of tune but it sometimes proves rather too inhibiting. The third violins can manage everything except the low E on the second crotchet of bar four. Surely the shade of Papa Haydn will be indulgent if we make it G instead. The next four bars are plain sailing. At bar eight there is a little section for wind alone. The original score runs like this:

Ex: 44

Our oboist will enjoy his solo here. We have not decided yet, by the way, what to do with our five clarinets. Perhaps the best thing is to keep the two inexperienced beginners mostly for the loud passages where they can each double one of the clarinet parts. This will give us one really good player and two reliable ones for the quieter bits. In this particular passage the second oboe part will be played by the first clarinet while the second and third can play Haydn's clarinet parts. As we have no bassoon the 'cellos will play the bassoon part omitting the semibreve F in bar six of the extract, resolving on E in bar seven. Here is something for our fourth and fifth clarinets. They can be trusted to do that anyway. They will play together in unison for confidence. All the clarinet parts will have to be transposed for B flat clarinets, of course (and the viola parts put into the treble clef for our third violins). The Gs for the horns in the last bar sound an octave lower than written, we must remember. They

Ex:45

can be given to the trumpets and trombones. It will be advisable to use two trumpets in unison as the tone will be fuller, though not necessarily louder, than that of a single trumpet. The passage will then stand as in our version on page 136.

Eight bars further on we encounter this passage: (The string parts are omitted)

The bassoon part here can be given to our first clarinet. As before, the trumpets and trombone are given the horn notes. A little later on there is a passage of twenty bars for wind alone in the course of which the following passage occurs:

This we shall arrange as before in the first three bars, i.e. first clarinet on the second oboe part, second and third clarinets on the clarinet parts and 'cellos on the bassoon part. At the fourth bar, in order to preserve Haydn's tone colour of oboe and clarinet in thirds in the fifth bar (and the three succeeding ones) we will give the oboe a crotchet G instead of letting him hold the tied semibreve. We will bring the flute in at bar four taking over the held G from the oboe, which is then ready to play Haydn's second oboe part. The last two bars will therefore appear thus:

Trumpets and trombone play the horn notes as before

The flute hands over to the oboe four bars later when the tune returns. The scoring will be the same as in Ex. 45 with the horns added. Ex. 49 shows the original scoring of the bar leading back to the tune and the opening two bars of it:

Our version (Ex. 50) shows the flute handing over to the oboe and the trumpet and trombone playing the horn parts. These are marked pp in comparison with the p of the horns.

At L begins the first fully scored passage in the movement. We give the bar leading in and four bars of *tutti*. The timpani and percussion parts (for triangle, bass drum and cymbals) are omitted to save space. Anyway they will be unchanged in our version. Here is the original scoring:

In the first bar of this extract the bassoons and violas are going to be sadly missed. We only have two 'cellos and one bass and a strong, sudden change of mood is essential here. We must add the trombone and be thankful that we have it. In bars two and three the trombone will play the second horn part, but in bars four and five it will perhaps be better to give it the bassoon part since our bass department is a little weak to support the *tutti*. The trumpets will play their part as written except for a G for the second player on the second minim of bar four. This replaces the G of the first horn in the original. The second oboe part will again be played by our first clarinet and Haydn's clarinet parts by our second and third. The fourth and fifth clarinets can also join in here as shown in our score. We have been fortunate so far with our third violin part on the whole and cannot complain that much of the viola part has been lost, though it is a pity about the first four notes of this extract being unattainable on the violin. It would be a mistake to give the violins the C and G and have to drop them out for the E flat and low C. Here is our version : (The brass and string parts are overleaf.)

There is rather an awkward place a little later on where the violas, 'cellos and basses are left alone to play this: (The rest of the orchestra have a sforzato G minim on the first beat.)

Ex: 53

Not only does the viola part go beyond the reach of our third violins, but the basses are written down to E flat which they cannot reach either. To deal with the basses first, it does not seem very pleasing for them to jump up a seventh from F to the upper E flat. We could either make them jump from the *sf* low G up to A flat a minor ninth higher, or get them up into the higher octave in the bar before. The latter seems more satisfactory as the leap is less noticeable when all the upper strings are playing.

It will be best to quote the string parts of the whole passage omitting the wind parts :

The bassoons double the 'cellos in the first two bars, then leap from the B up to the D a tenth above as we propose to do with our basses. We would therefore be justified in replacing the bassoon at that point by two of our clarinets. This would solve the problem of the viola F sharp at the end of bar three and we could also transfer the viola part in bars four and five to these same clarinets. We could use our third and fourth clarinets for this. We need the first and second for important duties beginning at bar five, hence the choice of third and fourth for this passage. The last three bars of the extract would therefore be arranged for the lower strings and third and fourth clarinets thus :

The violin parts would of course remain unchanged, so the descending character of the passage would be preserved owing to the ability of the 'cellos to go down to the E flat.

The following passage begins at the last bar of the above : (the percussion parts are again omitted)

The bassoon part is important. It is not well suited to the trombone; besides, that instrument is needed for the second horn part. Our third and fourth clarinets are already down in those regions and can take on the bassoon part. The first clarinet can play Haydn's clarinet part doubled in unison by the fifth clarinet, the second clarinet can take on the second oboe part. The strings need no alteration except the bass part in the first bar which, as we have seen, will have to be in unison not an octave below the 'cello for this one note, going down to low F in the next bar. The second trumpet will play the first horn part, the first trumpet part remaining unchanged. Our version of the wind parts will thus be :

Next time the main tune comes back it is scored for oboe accompanied by clarinets and bassoons exactly as before (Ex. 45)

K

but pizzicato chords on the strings are added and also a part for the two horns which goes like this (for the horns in C) in Haydn's score :

Ex: 58

We will give the first two bars to first trumpet and trombone and the rest of the passage to the two trumpets thus :

Ex: 59

A few bars later on a couple of low F sharps appear in the viola part in this string passage :

Ex: 60

The flute and clarinet are doubling the first and second violins respectively at the octave above, and it would be a pity to introduce clarinet tone among the string parts. We suggest the following for the third violins:

Ex: 61

3rd. Vln.

The D on the last beat of bar three is inserted to get the F sharp out of the way of the first violins now that is up in their register. It also makes the line more pleasing than dropping the major seventh from F sharp to G.

The following *tutti* in which the strings play the accompaniment to the wind poses some problems : (String parts overleaf.)

Ex:62

Fl.

Ob.

Cl. in C

Fg.

Hns. in C

Tpts. in C

The horns are badly missed here, also the bassoons. Without them the tune will be much weakened against the sonorous strings. We note, however, that the violins are outlining the melody much of the time which helps to bring it out. Our first clarinet will, as usual, play the second oboe part. Our second and third clarinets can have Haydn's clarinet parts, but can also supply some of the missing horn and bassoon notes. The fourth and fifth clarinets will be quite useful on the first bassoon and first horn parts, and the trombone, if he can be persuaded not to blast, will be able to take over the second horn and some of the second bassoon notes. We must keep Haydn's trumpet parts as they are. They are so typical of the period and any alteration of them would rob the score of most of its brightness. In the last bar the hopping bassoon part misses a great deal of its point on any other instrument, but we only have the 'cellos to do it and so have no choice. It may be better to use one 'cello only for this. This can be tried at rehearsal. The hopping part continues for half a dozen bars with a few wind instruments above it, so one 'cello should be enough and will probably sound neater than two. Our score will look like this : (The percussion players are all at work throughout.)

Ex:63

The two third violins are all that are left to cope with the horn parts in bars six and seven, but the violins are here outlining the tune in thirds, so that these two sustained violins will add body to them. The trombone may have to be told to play *mf* instead of *f* after the first two bars. It is wiser, by the way, to keep our fourth and fifth clarinets playing together in unison as much as possible, as they are inexperienced and not very expert players. All the members of the orchestra are naturally expected to practise their parts at home.

There is nothing else in this movement that will present any difficulty in the light of what we have already done. The violas' bottom C is used in a few bars:

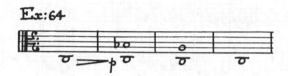

This need not cause any trouble as the low C is being held by the second horn (trombone in our version). Our third violins can therefore just play the B flat and A (which are important as they are not played at that pitch by any other instrument).

When as much cueing as this has to be done it is safer to write out the more difficult passages in score and draw the parts from it. For conducting purposes it may be more convenient, though laborious, to write the whole score out in the new version, but indications in red ink of who is playing what will usually be sufficient especially if (as is likely) the conductor has himself done the cueing.

We will now take extracts from various well-known works and see what can be done with them in the way of cueing or rearrangement for various incomplete combinations.

(1) Our orchestra consists of one of each of the wind instruments, flute, oboe, clarinet, bassoon horn, trumpet, trombone, timpani and one percussion player. We will imagine that they are all adequate performers and that we have a complete string section. The conductor has found that he can manage to cue down a fair number of works written for the classical orchestra,

but he and the players, some of whom are ballet-fans, would like to do some of the pieces from the *Casse-Noisette* Suite. On examining the score we can see at once that some of the numbers will have to be ruled out; these are No. 2 (a) *Marche*—too much exposed brass writing—No. 2 (e) *Danse Chinoise* urgently needs flute and piccolo playing together, also nothing can really replace the two bassoons keeping up their sepulchral noises all through, or the clarinets' double arpeggios. No. 2 (f) *Danse des Mirlitons* will not do for us either. It is three flutes or nothing for this, and there is also the brass section in the middle.

The rest should be possible, though some of it will be tricky to arrange. No. 1 *Ouverture Miniature,* scored for nine woodwind and two horns, triangle and violins and violas can probably be managed. No. 2 (b) *Danse de la Fée-Dragée* needs a celesta and a bass clarinet. We do not possess a celesta but our clarinettist has a bass clarinet and would be glad of a chance to give it an airing. It will present problems. The celesta part will have to be played on the piano, which is a pity, but a good player and instrument are available. No. 2 (c) *Danse Russe Trepak* is fully scored but the strings play the whole time and it should be possible to make it sound quite well. No. 2 (d) *Danse Arabe* is scored for woodwind and strings with tambourine. It contains a part for cor anglais. Our oboist does not possess one, but the part does not go below the bottom note of the oboe, and perhaps could sometimes be played by another instrument (e.g. muted horn). The first clarinet has a lot to do but the second and bass do not have very much. For No. 3 *Valse des Fleurs,* we shall have to call on the piano again, this time to play the harp part.

We have not the space to do more than pick out a few of the most difficult passages in each number and it will not be necessary to write out the cued-down version in score. Verbal directions only will be given here, but the reader with the help of the hints given ought to be able to work out a score for himself if he has the time. As in everything else the actual doing of the job is far more valuable than just reading instructions.

In the *Ouverture Miniature* Tchaikovsky writes for three flutes (third playing piccolo) and two each of the other woodwind and horns. The string parts will be left unchanged here and in all the pieces. The object is to try to reproduce the composer's scoring as closely as possible with our limited resources. The piccolo part can be largely dispensed with. It is mostly used to double in unison some of the high violin passages, but our flautist has a piccolo which he can change to if necessary. With the horns this makes eleven wind players. We have only four woodwind but we have a horn, a trumpet and a trombone which brings our wind force up to seven. We must be prepared to use the trumpet and trombone as skilfully and artistically as we can to fill up holes in the wind ensemble. Let us take this little scrap and see what can be done. No strings are playing :

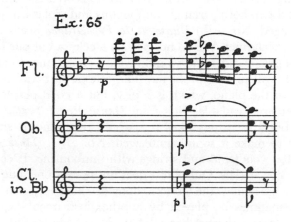

I feel that the second flute part should be kept in if possible. It is tempting to leave our flute alone on the top line, but it might sound rather thin. Our clarinet will therefore have to take the second flute part. This leaves us only with oboe and bassoon in our woodwind section. We could retain the first oboe part on our oboe, put the second clarinet notes on to the bassoon, the muted horn on the second oboe part and the muted trumpet on the first clarinet part.

If the top line were left to the flute only, the clarinet could play the first clarinet part and the muted trumpet the second oboe, leaving the horn out of it. This arrangement of the chord would sound better than the other we have suggested and there is a good deal to be said in favour of leaving out the second flute part after all; in fact I think we will settle for this. At letter B the wind is exposed, the violins having runs against it which we have omitted as they would be unaltered :

We obviously cannot have such densely packed harmony as this as we have not enough high-pitched instruments, but the

passage will lose its sparkle if we do not use the piccolo. The
flute has four bars rest before this passage and can therefore just
have time to change the piccolo so as to play the first flute part
(written an octave lower) up to the entry of the original piccolo
part. He will then switch over to this. Our part will therefore run
thus :

    As the first five bars would not be as strong as the same notes
on the flute we will mark it *f*, reverting to *mf* on the A flat so
as to make the crescendo up to *f* with the other instruments. We
proposed to retain the original first clarinet part until the last
quaver of bar 6, when our clarinet will switch to the second oboe
part, so the slightly colourless piccolo will be boosted up in the
opening bars by the clarinet at the lower octave. Our oboe will
play the original first oboe part in its entirety. Our trumpet will
play the second clarinet part, our bassoon the first bassoon part
and our horn the second bassoon (which happens here mostly to
be above the first). In this way the tune will be sufficiently prominent and will end up brilliantly, and the harmony will be complete without having to fall back on the trombone. The horn
and trumpet will not be muted but will be marked *p*, swelling up
to *mf* at the end. The piccolo will have fourteen more bars rest
in which to change back to flute. Later on the same passage
recurs in the recapitulation. Here Tchaikovsky's first flute
doubles the violins for four bars before, instead of having four
bars rest, but this can be omitted without being badly missed in
order to give time again for the change to piccolo. The rest of
this number will not give any trouble. There is much unison
doubling on the woodwind which can be replaced by single instruments.

    Danse de la Fée Dragée is more difficult because of the im-
portance of the bass clarinet and ordinary clarinet parts. We
have Tchaikovsky's permission to use the piano in place of celesta;

he puts *(ou piano)* in his score so our consciences are clear on that point. To return to the clarinet problem, if our clarinettist did not happen to possess a bass clarinet the important solo passages could be transferred to bassoon and this would make things easier. But whatever we do we must preserve the composer's scoring as closely as we can and the bass clarinet has such an individual sound that we must use it as we are fortunate enough to have one.

These well-known, bubbling passages come near the beginning of the piece and after that there is nothing important for the bass clarinet. The player can therefore take up his ordinary instrument again. The tricky passage (for our purpose) in which bass clarinet and both the others are all of importance runs as follows (The parts for the strings and celesta are omitted):

Here is our solution, starting at the bar before A :

The first little run is given to the flute *mf* so as not to cut short the low E on the bass clarinet which would happen if we gave the run to that instrument. After that the runs can be executed by the bass clarinet which thus replaces both Tchaikovsky's ordinary clarinets, the long notes at the ends of the runs being taken over by the horn. Our oboe plays the second flute part, trombone the cor anglais, and trumpet the first bassoon, while our bassoon plays the second bassoon part. The soft mutes (fibre) are specified on the brass. Metal mutes would sound too nasal, but the fibre mutes are admirable when a blend with woodwind is required.

The bass clarinettist now takes up his clarinet in A, as the bass clarinet is no longer needed. The corresponding passage at the end of the movement is all played on ordinary clarinets and there will be no difficulty in arranging the harmony with the help of muted trumpet (first oboe part), muted horn (cor anglais part) and bassoon (second oboe part).

We now come to the *Trepak*, No. 2 (c). It will be found that the wind and brass do a great deal of doubling of the string parts. With our limited supply of instruments we do not wish to waste any of them on this doubling work when there is something more important for them to do. The composer's scoring and the rhythmic verve and accent which make this piece so effective must be carried out to the best of our ability with the resources we have. Our three brass instruments will have to be worked pretty hard, for they have to represent horns in the less fully scored portions and heavy brass elsewhere. Tchaikovsky, as usual, frequently writes his four horns in two parts, two horns to a part, and the trumpet and horn can be put on to those parts, the trombone being kept, so far as possible, for passages where the composer uses trombones in his score. It will probably be best in the *tutti* to give our trombones the bass trombone part.

Where the first flute plays an octave above the first violins it must also do so in our cued version, otherwise much brilliance will be lost. There are certain things which must be brought out strongly, for instance at bar five of the piece this passage occurs. We have put it into short score to save space and because it is simple enough in texture :

The thirds at the top of the wind reduction are played only by flutes, and they are put in to give an element of smoothness to the violin parts. The lower notes (C, B etc.) are not played by the strings and are given prominence by being scored for cor anglais, two clarinets and bass clarinet, a sonorous combination. The fifths in the bass staff of the wind are played by the two bassoons.

I would suggest putting the thirds on flute and oboe, with the oboe on the top part because it is more penetrating than the flute. It is unnecessary to use our bassoon on the off-beat fifths—violas, 'celli divisi and basses are sufficient for them. We can then use the rich unison combination of clarinet, bassoon and horn for the middle part, which is quite a fair substitute for Tchaikovsky's scoring though the nuttiness of the cor anglais tone will be missed. The horns come in with three D's *piano*, on the first three quavers of bar four of the extract. The trumpet can do this.

At letter B the following passage occurs. It is at the beginning of a section in which the main thematic interest is transferred to the bass:

In the condensed score on page 158 the instrumentation is this :

Line 1. Three flutes.

Line 2. Oboes, cor anglais, clarinets.

Line 3. Horns (shown here at actual pitch).

Line 4. Violins, alternate firsts and seconds playing triple stops.

Line 5. Bassoons, bass clarinet, violas, 'cellos and basses.

The difficulty is to decide what to do with Line 2. Line 1 will have to be left to one flute on the top part only. The chords on the violins give a strongly marked rhythm and our single flute will brighten up the off-beats. (Rather surprisingly Tchaikovsky does not use a piccolo in this number.) We shall have to take our bassoon off line 5 and use it and the oboe and clarinet on line 2. As, presumably, our strings are at less than full symphonic strength there is some chance of line 2 being heard. Actually it is never very prominent in the original scoring, the effect of which is mainly the strong quaver rhythm on the violins and a not very clear but nevertheless exciting scramble in the bass. The horns help to give substances and firmness to the texture (Line 3). There are two horns on the first note and two on each part after that. We will use our horn and trombone for this. The trumpet will not be needed at all here.

In the final *tutti* (two bars after *stringendo*) we find the following lay-out. Again we give it in condensed score; two bars will suffice as the scoring remains the same up to the end : (Ex. 72.)

The lines are distributed among the orchestra thus:

Line 1 :   Violins and flutes.
Line 2 :   Oboes.
Line 3 :   Violas, 'cellos, horns one and two.
Line 4 :   Trumpets, the rhythm reinforced by tambourine.
Line 5 :   Trombones one and two, horns three and four.
Line 6 :   Bassoons, bass clarinet, bass trombone, tuba, double basses and timpani.

We will take our flute off line 1 and put it on to the top part of line 2. Our oboe will play the lower part of these thirds (the

original second oboe part). Our horn and bassoon will play the
thirds in line 3, our trumpet the first trumpet part (line 4), our
trombone line 5, and we only have the double basses and timpani for line 6. The timpani are playing the fifth, G and D on
two drums, which makes a great deal of noise, so we shall not
miss the other bass instruments too much.

No. 2 (d) *Danse Arabe.* Scored for woodwind (three flutes, two
oboes and cor anglais, two clarinets and bass clarinet and two
bassoons), tambourine and muted strings. Here is the opening
woodwind phrase :

The cor anglais part transposed down a fifth will be played by
the oboe. This will sound coarser than the cor anglais, but retains
the reedy, exotic tone colour of the original to a large extent
though a good balance is not so easy to get. If at rehearsal the
oboe were found to be too prominent a muted horn (fibre mute)
could be used instead. It would depend a good deal on the oboist,
his reed and his instrument. The second clarinet part will be
played by our bassoon. Later on the same passage recurs with
bassoons substituted for clarinets. The cor anglais plays the same
part as before. In this instance we will put the bassoon on the
top line and the clarinet on the second bassoon part, using the
oboe for the cor anglais part as before.

There are some long held fifths, low G and D held softly by
two clarinets. Our flute can take the D. At letter B the two
bassoons have a duet, mainly in thirds, against the strings. We
will use our bassoon on the original first bassoon part, clarinet

L

on the second. The part is well within the clarinet's low register. Later on there is a short solo for cor anglais which, luckily, goes down to the bottom note of the oboe and no further, so we can use our oboe for that.

The following descending phase is score for contrasted families of woodwind :

Ex: 74

The two chords marked " a " are on three flutes, " b " are on oboes and cor anglais, " c " are on clarinets and bass clarinet. We must keep the original instruments at the top of each pair of chords of course; the chords could be arranged in this way (in order of pitch) :

    (a)   Flute, oboe, clarinet.
    (b)   Oboe, flute, clarinet.
    (c)   Clarinet, horn, bassoon.

I have suggested the horn because it blends so well with clarinet and bassoon. The only woodwind instrument available for the C and B flat would have been the oboe which would stick out like a sore thumb at that pitch. When this passage comes later an octave lower the chords marked " z " give trouble because of our lack of a bass clarinet and second bassoon :

Ex: 75

The chords are arrranged as follows, again in order of pitch :

   (x)   Flute, cor anglais, oboe.
   (y)   Clarinets and bass clarinet.
   (z)   Bassoon 1, bass clarinet, bassoon 2.

We will score chords " x " and " y " for flute, oboe and clarinet and for clarinet horn and bassoon respectively. Much as we
should like to put the bassoon at the top of the " z " pair of
chords it would leave us with no choice for the lower parts than
horn and trombone. No other instruments that we have in our
limited ensemble can get down there. If we use our clarinet at
the top, the horn can take the middle part and the bassoon the
bottom. It is rather a growly part for the horn, but should sound
adequate as it is embedded between the other two instruments
and not too much exposed.

Our arrangement would therefore be:

The timbre of the clarinet is so different at " y " and " z " that
a substantial contrast has been achieved after all.

Finally there is the eerie effect of the two bassoons in octaves, dying away at the end to *ppppp* :

This could be done by transferring the first bassoon part to the flute, the bassoon playing the lower part or, if it were thought more desirable to retain the strange individual sound of the high bassoon, the lower octave could be given to the clarinet, or even the muted horn (fibre mute). Experiments could be made at rehearsal to decide which is best. Personally I think the bassoon on the top and the clarinet underneath would probably be the most satisfactory arrangement, but if our bassoonist were scared of such exposed high notes (though they are not excessively high) it would be safer to adopt the first suggestion, using the flute.

No. 3. *Valse des Fleurs.*

The opening chords are written thus :

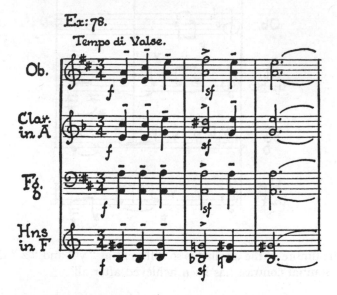

These could be cued as follows :

> Oboe 2 to Flute.
>
> Clarinet 2 to Horn *(mf)*.
>
> Bassoon 2 to Bassoon.
>
> Horn 1 to Trumpet *(mf)*.
>
> Horn 2 to Trombone *(mf)*.

The A on Bassoon 1 is not indispensable and can be left out with little loss to the general effect.

Later on four horns are used in a similar passage. It will be necessary to decide which notes can be dispensed with without leaving out any essential notes or producing top-heavy spacing.

When we come to the waltz itself the horns play :

Nothing can truly replace this horn quartet. Our horn will of course play the first horn part. Our clarinet will take over the third, bassoon the second and trombone the fourth. A good trombonist can produce something not unlike horn tone and clarinet and bassoon can always be trusted to blend well with horns. At letter B the bass trombone and horns play the accompaniment to the strings with little interpolations on the woodwind :

We cannot get all these notes in through sheer lack of instruments. The horn chords can be played by trumpet (horn one), horn (horn three) and trombone (horn two). Our bassoon will play the bass trombone part *mf* or even *f*. The fourth horn part will have to be left out. The first flute, first oboe and first clarinet parts will be played; second flute, second clarinet and first bassoon will have to be omitted. Somewhat thinner than the original it is true, but if they really play *ff* it should pass muster. Sixteen bars before letter E the clarinets and bassoons hold quiet background chords:

Against these chords the flute and oboe play the tune in octaves while two solo strings have runs in quavers. The harp supplies the waltz rhythm and two basses reinforce the first beats. This scheme continues for another twenty-six bars. Our orchestra can therefore supply everything as in the original score except these chords, but they can be arranged (going down in order of pitch) for clarinet, horn, trombone and bassoon. As the clarinets and bassoons are interlocked or " dove-tailed " this means that the horn will play the first bassoon part and the trombone the second clarinet. The horn and trombone will have to play " open ", not muted notes because they will have just been taking part in a loud passage and there will not be time to insert the mutes. True, the horn could hand-stop his notes but that is not the kind of muted effect we want. If they both play really softly the result will be satisfactory. The next section, in B minor, will go well if the trombone is used for the lower horn part (the four horns are written in two-part harmony). At letter G the wind parts are of the pattern on page 169. (Ex. 82.)

Since the first and second violins have the melody we can (reluctantly) dispense with the piccolo, the runs on the flute being essential. Our bassoon can have the second clarinet part as the basses are playing the bassoon part pizzicato, which is sufficient. This pattern continues for several bars but the second clarinet part never goes too high for the bassoon so all will be well, though the gilt-edge given to the violins by the piccolo is certainly a loss. As there is no harp part for the piano to play just here, the piccolo part (plus the octave below) might be put in by the pianist quietly and discreetly.

At letter H the four-horn theme returns with the waltz rhythm on trombones and tuba. As the strings, apart from 'cellos and basses on the first beats, are silent they can take over this duty.

Another difficult problem arises mid-way between letters I and K:

Ex. 83 (Continued)

If we put the horn and trombone on to the waltz-rhythm we
are depriving the main theme of too much of its power. The
piano will be a good deal louder than the harp, and so will be
very useful here. We can also give the 'cellos and basses the
rhythm thus:

For the rest we will keep the first oboe part, give our clarinet the second clarinet part, keep the first bassoon part, give our horn the second oboe part, keep the first trumpet part and give our trombone the second bassoon part.

When the same passage returns a little later in F major, Tchaikovsky does not use the harp and he also adds the 'cellos to the violas in the string countermelody, but we can use the piano and 'cellos as before for the rhythm. The wind and brass parts turn out to be easier to cue than in the D major version. Here is our cued score of the wind and brass parts:

Ex:85

Our oboe plays the original second oboe part. We have given the first oboe part to the clarinet, as being more powerful than the oboe at that pitch. Our bassoon is a composite of the original bassoon parts, our horn plays the third horn part, we keep the first trumpet part and give the trombone the second horn part.

The rest of the piece should not pose any serious problems. The string writing is mostly pretty full and there is a good deal of doubling between the wind instruments in chords. When the resources available are inadequate to provide a satisfactory ensemble the use of a piano is imperative. But to get real musical pleasure and interest both the piano part and the parts played by what instruments there are should be carefully edited. If there are, say, three flutes, two clarinets and a trumpet, none of them very expert, and four or five violins and a 'cello, also not too reliable, it should be possible by choosing simple music and calling on the help of an alert and intelligent, not necessarily technically brilliant pianist to obtain with patience and imagination some result not entirely painful. In an instance like this the first prerequisite from the piano is a firm bass. The pianist should avoid reduplicating parts which are being played by such instruments as are present and concentrate on missing parts unless of course the ensemble is so rocky that it needs solid support all the way in the old continuo manner. There are, fortunately, ever decreasing examples in schools of lamentably thin and unbalanced assemblages of instruments calling themselves " the school orchestra ". There has been occasion earlier in this book to remark upon the interest shown by boys and girls in wind instruments and also in that still comparatively rare bird the viola. But the necessity for cueing very often arises and enough has been said about that subject to show that it is better to have, say, an oboe solo played by a flute or clarinet than to leave it to the piano, and that brass instruments carefully used, with or without mutes, can take certain parts originally written for woodwind, especially supporting chords. Knowledge of the individual abilities of members of the orchestra comes into the matter of cueing as it does also into the choice of music. An orchestra without horns would hardly choose the Nocturne from Mendelssohn's *Midsummer Night's Dream* music. Speaking of horns, I believe that horn parts have been played on saxophones occasionally in incomplete orchestras, but I have not heard the effect of this. The jazz style with vibrato would have to be severely checked in the first place and also it might be difficult to attain satisfactory blend and balance with the other instruments. That is the trouble with saxophones in normal symphony orchestras and supplies the reason why they are used, if at all, as solo instruments, and rarely as integral parts of the wind ensemble.

If there is a fairly large body of strings and only a few wind instruments these may be implemented by piano duet (four hands on one piano). Again, this must be arranged with taste and artistic judgment, so that the pianists do not pound away the whole time. Better still would be two players on two pianos, one kept for the fully scored passages. If instruments are available percussion players can usually be found. This is a fruitful way of developing musicianship, but of course it would be an artistic error of the first magnitude to introduce percusssion instruments not in the score just for the sake of employing players.

In the next chapter we will take odd passages from suitable works and try to find out how to get the most out of still more limited resources, using the piano.

CHAPTER X

FURTHER EXAMPLES OF CUEING, USING
PIANOFORTE

LET US imagine we have at our disposal two flutes, an oboe, two trumpets and a trombone with timpani and any other percussion that may be required. Our few wind players are not absolute beginners and are keen and willing to practise their parts. With a combination like this, however skilful we may be at cueing, a piano will be necessary if we are to tackle even the simplest symphonic music. The thing to aim at, all the same, is to do without the pianoforte wherever possible. There are not many works which only use one trombone, but there is one very attractive one, Glinka's *Kamarinkaya*, which only requires a bass trombone. Ours is a tenor, but no doubt he will be able to manage quite well as the compasses of tenor and bass trombones are not very different from one another. Our strings are not bad because we have confident leaders in each section who carry the others with them.

The work is scored for double woodwind, two horns in D, two trumpets in F, trombone, timpani and strings. As we have three 'cellos one of them can be used on any important bassoon passages that may occur. We will write out a special composite part for him as we do not want to weaken our 'cello section when he is not needed for playing bassoon cues. It may not, however, be necessary to use him much as a bassoon as we have a trombonist who is supplied with mutes as are also our two trumpeters.

We will only take a few examples which appear to present special difficulties.

Here is a little woodwind passage:

Only one flute is used here. This sets our second flute free to play the second clarinet part. The first clarinet is doubling the flute to begin with in unison, so that it can be dispensed with. The only real difficulty comes in bar four where the second clarinet goes above the first and the first has the most important line, but if we leave out the first three quavers of the oboe part in this bar (they are doubled by the bassoon an octave lower) the oboe can take the first clarinet, the second flute continuing with the second clarinet and our trumpet can complete the oboe part. If he is a very reliable player he can play the missing three oboe quavers too, but it would probably be safer not. He will of course be muted. The bassoon part will be played by our roving 'cello. Our version will thus be:

Some adjustments of dynamics may be necessary, the oboe for instance may be too prominent at *mf*, while the muted trumpet may be too soft at *p*.

There is a delightful passage later on, which we need not quote, in which the oboe holds on F (top line) doubled by bassoon an octave lower in syncopated crotchets while the clarinet plays the principal tune. The oboe we have, the bassoon note could be given to the muted trumpet and our first flute could play the clarinet part. The clarinet is then joined by the bassoon against a pizzicato string accompaniment whilst the flute plays an independent counterpoint above. The piano would have to be used here as seen in our example and would continue during the ensuing *tutti* a few bars of which are shown. In bars seven and eight of the extract the strings play double stops. The chords on the top staff fit our three wind and three brass instruments. In bar nine the piano represents clarinets and bassoons in the original score.

There are some *tutti* passages later on where the piano could
add its weight with advantage but it is surprising to find how few

passages really need it and how little of the effect of the original would be lost by using our six wind instruments instead of Glinka's thirteen. I may add that this work was chosen simply because it has only one trombone. The other instruments were selected at random without consulting the score to see whether they would fit the piece and with the expectation that a great deal more cueing and use of piano would be necessary than was found to be the case. Of course the devices to which we have now become accustomed of using a trumpet and a trombone to represent horns (or sometimes two trumpets if the horn parts are high enough) would have to be used, and there are some places where trumpets, sometimes muted, sometimes not, could play missing woodwind parts. Our roving 'cello would not need to function as a bassoon very much. In this little passage (against a held D in harmonics on the strings) it would be more satisfactory to use the two muted trumpets on the clarinet thirds rather than the oboe and a muted trumpet. Parallel thirds like this are best when each pair of thirds is of uniform tone-colour :

The absence of flutes is a serious handicap. There is no other instrument which can replace it in the higher part of its compass where it spends so much of its time doubling the violins or other wind instruments at the octave above.

The oboe or clarinet can get up fairly high but only if they are really good players can they be relied upon for good and steady tone among the leger lines. Of course if there is a pair of oboes or even an oboe and clarinet there are eighteenth-century works written for oboes, horns and/or bassoons and strings which could be used. It need not be considered lacking in scholarship or

M

purity of style to use clarinets instead of oboes, or an oboe and a clarinet for two oboes, as we are assured by musical historians that eighteenth-century composers were not as fussy about what played what as we are. Handel wrote overtures and such-like pieces for two clarinets and horns, and the use of clarinets in his music and that of his contemporaries is therefore not strictly anachronistic. But a programme or an orchestral practice concerned only with music of a limited period and style may easily become boring and most players will want to take part in works of varied character.

It is only possible for such orchestras as we have been considering to play music written in very straightforward idioms unless of course pieces are written specially for them, taking into account the varied abilities of the players. Much late nineteenth- and twentieth-century music is written either for large orchestras which it would be impossible to reduce except in small details, or demands professional competence of a high standard from the players.

Composers of our own and recent times use instrumental colour as an indispensable and essential factor in their musical language and it would entirely destroy the point of their works to cue them for other instruments. Other points too are the necessity for the utmost purity of intonation in music based on the free use of dissonance and the confidence which makes each player know that he is playing the right note at the right time even if no one else is.

But to return to our flutes, or rather our lack of them, we will assume that we have a pair of oboes, a clarinet, a bassoon, a horn, two trumpets and timpani. It would be wise to confine ourselves to works written without trombones. Our strings are competent enough to give a reasonable account of the easier works of the classical period. A Beethoven overture is suggested as the opening item of the next concert. *Egmont* needs four horns, not to mention a piccolo, and the *Leonora* uses trombones. *Coriolanus* is not very easy, but all the better—it gives something to work at with its cross rhythms and so on and it is a splendid example of middle-period Beethoven at his best, also it is written for normal woodwind, two horns, two trumpets and timpani. Of course it would be possible to engage one or even a pair of flautists, but it has always been the policy of our orchestra to rely entirely, for good or ill, on its own resources. These resources include a pianist for whom we shall either write out a part or go through the score with him marking what he is to play.

The opening can be left to the orchestra. The chords will be full enough on the strings (both violins will have triple-stopped chords) and what wind we have.

We give the first four bars in short score to remind the reader of how the overture begins:

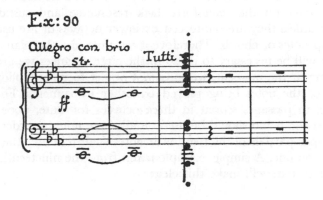

There are five crashing chords like this and although the flutes have higher notes than any of the other instruments in some of them their absence will not be missed to any very noticeable extent. We will keep the trumpets to Beethoven's parts here and probably throughout the work except when one of them is possibly needed to supply an important note on one of the missing instruments. Beethoven uses the open C of the C trumpets with magnificently bold effect in several places in this overture against chords to which that note is foreign, or at any rate only distantly related. An instance of this occurs in the second big chord at the seventh bar of the work in which the trumpets' C appears in the middle of a diminished seventh chord on F. Theorists might say that this turns the chord into a dominant eleventh, but if so it is in a very peculiar inversion and position! The point is that we must be careful to preserve all dissonant elements of this kind, otherwise we shall find ourselves bowdlerising and emasculating the music, which is the last thing we want to do. With regard to the missing flute parts, although the upward compass of the oboe extends to G on the fourth leger line it is useless to expect our first oboe to supply that note as a flute cue, or indeed any note above, say D above the staff. The highest notes of the oboe are difficult to produce and are thin in quality, having none of the ability of the flute at that pitch to give brightness to the top ranges of the orchestra. The pianoforte can do that much better, but I feel that if the pianoforte is needed for this purpose it is rather feeble just to give it the flute notes alone. High notes on the pianoforte lack resonance and sustaining power unless they are reinforced by lower octaves or are used as the top notes of chords. Therefore if we must use the pianoforte and it will be necessary to do so in the circumstances we are envisaging at the moment, we must not object to its reduplicating some of the notes being played by other instruments. For instance, in passages scored in three octaves for flute, oboe and clarinet the piano should be used on all three notes in order that the upper partials of the two lower notes shall reinforce the tone of the top one. A simple example taken from the nineteenth and twentieth bars will make this clear :

A few bars later this passage shows the use of the pianoforte in chords. Not only does this method give the high notes of the pianoforte more chance of competing with the orchestra but it also fills in any thinness that might result from the absence of the other missing instruments besides the flutes :

Before giving the suggested pianoforte part for this passage (in which the strings are also taking part) we had better decide what to do with our single clarinet bassoon and horn. In the second bar of the extract the clarinets and horns double each other at the unison, therefore the clarinet can stick to the first clarinet notes while the horn plays the second horn part. The 'cellos, basses and second violas have the bass of the passage, so the bassoon will be more useful if it plays the first basoon part.

The piano will play this :

The horns and/or trumpets have to stop playing for a few bars in what would otherwise be *tutti* because their open notes will not fit in with the harmony. It may be tempting when there are missing instruments to give them something to play in these bars but this temptation must be resisted as being out of style and period. Care should be taken about whether our single instruments shall play the original first or second part at any given point, so as to make sure that our instruments are not being wasted by unison or octave doubling where as full harmony as possible is wanted.

There is a long-held (ten bars) octave in B flat for the horns under the second subject which acts as a kind of sustaining pedal to the arpeggio accompaniment of the 'cellos. Our horn can take the low B flat and one of the trumpets the upper one which will be a nice note, middle C, for our B flat trumpet.

A few bars later on we come to a long-held C on the flute (seven bars). This would of course soon disappear on the piano and it would be inartistic to strike it every bar or two bars to keep it going. Fortunately this note is within easy reach of the oboe which can very neatly take it over. (Ex. 94.)

Our oboe can switch to the flute part at bar four of the extract while the pianoforte, having played the flute part with the

Ex. 94 (Continued)

hands two octaves apart (the left hand with the bassoon), finishes off with the oboe part in bars four and five. The bassoon, after playing the first bassoon part as far as the G in bar four, will drop to the second bassoon's low C and so we shall have the sustained C on our four woodwind instruments. There is another passage where the piano can be dispensed with as a flute-substitute. I quote the woodwind parts only:

Ex: 95

The most satisfactory way of cueing this would be to transfer our oboe to the original flute part and give Beethoven's oboe part to our first clarinet, thus avoiding taking the clarinet any higher than necessary. Our second clarinet will play the second bassoon part, our bassoon the first. The strings are playing but none of the woodwind notes is being doubled by them so it is important that this little passage should be complete on our woodwind.

Single notes on the pianoforte, not octaves, would be suitable for little flute passages like the following :

The reader may ask " Why not use your oboe for this flute passage?" The answer is that this is the beginning of an extended sequential passage which takes the flute up to F and I feel that it would be inartistic to use the oboe where the notes are within its reach and the piano later on in exactly the same motif just because it has gone inconveniently high for the oboe. Here our bassoon would play the second bassoon part and our second clarinet the first.

Where the flute is doubling the violins in unison it is unnecessary to use the piano. In the following extract although it is a loud passage the first violins are so powerful that the flute is not much missed. The rest of the wind is essential and we have the instruments necessary for satisfactory harmony, though one or other of the bassoon parts will have to be omitted. The bass is somewhat weakened if the bassoon is taken off it, but the 'cellos give it a good send-off on the first beat so we will decide to give our bassoon the first bassoon part. The only other instrument

Example 97

that has the same notes is the oboe two octaves higher and the E
natural going to F is very essential to the harmony. (Ex. 97, on
page 185.)

On the return of the second subject in C major Beethoven uses
his second bassoon as a second-horn to hold the long G corresponding to the long B flat held note we quoted before. His second
horn holds the note at the higher octave. We can do exactly the
same, but our first clarinet will have to play the first bassoon part
when it comes in with the melody in octaves with the oboe. The
wind parts only are quoted : (From the original score.)

Later on, the following bar is repeated four times. The piano
will have been playing in the previous eight bar *tutti* and it may
be found that, if it did not continue, too much loss of tone would
result. But I do not think that is likely as the drums and trumpets
also stop playing at this point :

Example 99

In the repetitions the double bass F is played an octave higher. There is no other change.

In our version the first clarinet can play the flute part and the bassoon can easily manage both bassoon parts. We could put one of our trumpets on the first horn and our horn on the second. In this way no notes are left out. There are no more problems in what remains of the work. There is another long high C held by the flutes for ten bars, but Beethoven's first oboe has it too, with the first violins playing the same note in a rhythmical pattern, and with trumpets and clarinets holding or also playing rhythms on C in octaves below, so that nothing needs to be done about it. In fact our piano which has not had to work very hard after all is hardly needed any more.

Enough has been said about this matter of cueing down to show the sort of problems that occur and suggest some solutions. Even if circumstances never arise which make it necessary to undertake this arduous but rewarding task, the exercise of cueing is a valuable part of the study of orchestration for not only does it develop ingenuity but also gives a detailed insight into the methods of the masters whose scores we need to subject to the minute inspection necessary to carry out the work in an artistic way. This is a purely technical task, it is not creative though it calls for intelligent musicianship. There must never be any idea of altering or "improving" existing orchestration. The composer's intentions must be honestly carried out to the limits of the possibilities of the available resources. Careful and sensitive cueing will express the composer's ideas far more closely than just handing out parts for the instruments you have and " filling in " on the piano.

When writing large works requiring a high standard of virtuosity from the players, composers do not usually feel that their ideas can be adequately clothed in less expensive and voluminous raiment, though sometimes they may cue in essential parts written for the more exotic instruments for those in more general use. But in writing, for instance, orchestral accompaniments for cantatas designed for, or within the scope of, small choral societies or schools it is wise to demand a minimum of instruments as a possible basis. The most satisfactory results are obtained by writing for this indispensable minimum and adding parts for other instruments to play if they are there. For instance, the minimum could be five woodwind (two clarinets), two horns, two trumpets, percussion and strings with possibly a harp part which could be played on the piano. Afterwards the other three woodwind, another pair of horns, three trombones and tuba can be added. Even if composers are unpractical in their early days they have to learn to adapt themselves to real-life conditions as they go on. They cannot expect Ludwigs of Bavaria to finance them in these days, and they find it wiser to see what they can do without rather than how much they can use unless they do not mind whether their works are performed or not.

CHAPTER XI

SOME GENERAL PRINCIPLES OF ORCHESTRATION

THE FIRST prerequisite for the would-be writer for the orchestra or any other combination of instruments is to be able to recognise instantly the sound of any instrument at all its possible ranges of pitch. Some instruments vary in timbre so much in different parts of their compass that they almost seem different instruments. This is particularly true of the clarinet and bassoon. The chalumeau register of the clarinet sounds very different from the pure limpid sounds of the medium or the shrill hard tone of the top register. Similarly the highest notes of the bassoon bear little relation to the low ones. Most instruments become louder or at any rate more penetrating as they rise in pitch, but the double-reeds (oboe and bassoon families) behave in the opposite way. It is difficult to play really softly at the bottom of their compass. This is why a bass clarinet is usually substituted for a bassoon in the well-known descending phrase in Tchaikovsky's *Pathétique*. Clarinets of all sizes can play extremely quietly even up to a considerable height when played by performers of professional excellence.

Opportunities for listening and absorbing the sounds of instrumental combinations are abundant. Gramophone recordings are extremely faithful (usually) in their reproductions and broadcast music of all kinds is poured out every day. The study of scores is not only immensely valuable to the student of the orchestra, but is absolutely essential, for though he should not wish to take other people's ideas but to develop his own for what they are worth the only way of becoming a good orchestrator is to culti-vate the power of mental hearing. This can only be done by assimilating orchestral sounds until any can be imagined at will, even those made by combinations never actually heard. Better than any mechanical devices is, naturally, attendance at concerts. But those who do not live within a reasonable radius from a symphony orchestra may have to depend on gramophone and radio mainly for their musical sustenance. The study of scores also teaches normal methods of using the orchestra, and abnormal ones too. The former lay the foundation of a sound technique, the latter stimulate and excite the imagination and show fresh ways of doing things.

Neat musical handwriting should be cultivated assiduously. Conductors are very conscientious in examining scores with a view to possible performance but they are only human as well as not having all the time in the world at their disposal. It is too much to expect them to spend hours in deciphering untidy and ill-spaced scores. Scores should be written neatly in ink, not in pencil, and should contain ample rehearsal letters or numbers. Clefs should be written at the beginning of every page, not on the left hand only. There is a strong movement in favour of writing and printing scores with the transposing instruments at their sounded pitch (i.e. " in C "). This method is particularly favoured by serial composers so that the eye can the more easily take in the structural basis of the music. It is possible that the time may come when players themselves are taught their instruments on non-transposing lines. But at present if their parts are written at sounded pitch the onus of transposition is thrown on them. This does not trouble professional experts very much but would certainly worry amateurs.

Extremes of pitch, high pitch especially, should be avoided except for brief passages. It is not the occasional high note or high episode that causes players discomfort but it is when the general lie (tessitura) of a part lies high that they find it taxing. These remarks apply to wind rather than string players though these do not care to spend their whole time in the high positions.

It is not necessary to be able to play the instruments you write for but it is desirable to understand their technique to some extent so as to avoid writing excessively awkward parts for them. Many successful composers have been indifferent performers, indeed, composition has become so complex an art that composers

need to specialise in it. There are notable exceptions of course
but on the whole composers are not outstanding as executants
nor as conductors even of their own works. Sound and valuable
advice and information about the technique and capabilities of
all the instruments are given in larger treatises on orchestration,
notably those of Forsyth and more recently Walter Piston, and
much can be gained from even chance remarks dropped by
players and of course by the study of scores. A little ability to
play an instrument may have an inhibiting effect by engender-
ing too timid an attitude towards difficulties.

Phrasing marks for wind and bowing for strings must be carefully thought out and written in to the score. String players do
not always take the same view of the most effective or practicable
method of bowing a passage and often suggest slight alterations
to which it is wise for the non-string player to give respectful
consideration, but the composer or orchestrator must indicate the
broad outlines of bowing or he will not have his music performed
in the style he has in mind. Marks of expression and dynamics
are also frequently too sparse in the works of inexperienced
writers. The way a passage should go may seem unmistakable to
the writer but not to the player reading the music for the first
time. It is hardly possible to be too minutely particular in this way.
An orchestral player has only his own part before him and has
no idea until he has played in the work several times what the
other instruments are doing or what general effects are intended.
His part must therefore contain as explicit directions as possible.
Notation cannot, of course, indicate every nuance of phrasing
and tone. Orchestral players and conductors are musicians with
instinctive feelings for such things but the composer should have
a clear idea of how he really wants the music to sound and the
ability to write such signs and directions as will be instantly
grasped and complied with by the orchestra. Saving of time at
rehearsal is an all-important consideration too, and a well-
marked score and parts helps greatly towards this most desirable
end.

The necessity for economy in the use of extra instruments and
players has already been stressed and the wisdom of cueing
essential passages written for the less commonly used instruments
into the parts for the standard ones is obvious. Some works are

written for the sheer pleasure of writing them without much thought of performance. No mundane practical considerations should be allowed to inhibit the full expression of an artist's creative personality. But most composers wish to communicate their ideas and not merely work in a self-centred vacuum and if they are to realise this aim it is inadvisable, to put it mildly, to clutter up their scores with a lot of expendable and expensive apparatus.

Experience of orchestral playing from the inside is tremendously useful to a composer even if he only wields the humble triangle beater or cymbals, better still if he plays one of the more important instruments. He gets from this experience a knowledge of music from the performers' point of view and from the point of view of the orchestral player in particular. Orchestral musicians are artists with a high regard for minutiæ of their craft, and apart from the valuable lessons that can be learned from sitting in an orchestra and observing and listening to all that goes on at rehearsal and performance, the comments and criticisms one hears, often salted with sardonic wit, from one's fellow members of the band are in themselves a liberal musical education.

Orchestral players are quick to detect whether a composer really understands their instruments, and one who is able to show by his use of them that he has this understanding and is writing for them as well as for himself and his audience will go a long way to securing their generous interest and co-operation. An orchestra is not just an assemblage of instruments, it is composed of as varied a collection of human beings as can be found anywhere except that they are bound together by a common dedication to the ideal of perfection in making music. They expect conductors and connoisseurs to be exacting in their attitude to them, and in turn they subject their own conductors, the soloists whom they accompany and the composers whose music they play to equally stern criticism.

When it comes to actual performance one of the most important factors in ensuring smooth and equable rehearsal is an accurate and legible set of parts. Paying for the copying of parts is a costly business and it may have to be a case of " do it yourself ".

If the composer has not first-hand knowledge of how a well

N

laid-out band part should look he will be well advised to examine
some parts written by a good professional copyist, observing
especially how rests are written, cues are given and a few bars'
rest allowed for turning the pages over, especially in wind and
percussion parts which are not shared, as are string parts, by
two players. Parts should not be written in small notes on
narrow-meshed music paper. The bigger the notes the better. I
remember a player once saying " I like a minim to look like a
real fat minim ". Tails should always be joined to the heads of
the notes.

It is not good scoring constantly to give strings and wind exactly the same notes to play. A certain amount of such doubling
is of course unavoidable and is even desirable in fully scored
passages. But it is often far better, for instance, to give the wind
sustained chords (where the nature of the music permits this) in
support of rhythmic repetition of the same chords by the strings.
It is part of the nature of wind instruments to sustain and strings
to move as we have seen from some of the musical examples given
in earlier pages of this book.

When scoring vocal accompaniments great care is needed not so
much for fear of drowning the voice as of making the words in-
audible. In opera, where the singers are well above the level of
the orchestra the words and notes often come through scoring
which would drown them in a concert hall. Wind and percussion
can obscure the words far more easily than strings, but of course
it is impossible really to give any hard and fast advice because
singers differ so much between themselves in strength of voice
and clearness of enunciation. A great deal depends on the pitch
of the vocal part and the actual syllables being sung. Though
effective examples could be quoted of the opposite procedure it is
better as a general principle not to reduplicate the vocal line in
the orchestra. Study of the full score of a work like *The Dream
of Gerontius* would be a help in this matter. There is plenty of
colour and contrast in the accompaniments to the solo voices but
Elgar has restrained his natural orchestral exuberance there just
as he did in his 'cello concerto. The 'cello is very easily covered
up especially in its medium register, but every note it plays in
this concerto can be clearly heard although a full orchestra is
used. The violin naturally comes through an orchestral texture

more easily. Its high registers are penetrating and its G string tone powerful. It is a remarkable phenomenon that a single violin can stand out against an accompaniment containing thirty or more violins. In all orchestral accompanying, the marks of dynamics have mostly to be kept at a considerably lower level than those of the soloist whether vocal or instrumental, except in piano concertos, and even then it will depend on the fullness or otherwise of the brass writing whether the piano is clearly heard. As in all matters which concern the art of orchestration it is the nature of the music itself and whether it has been conceived orchestrally from the beginning which is an important factor in its ultimate effectiveness. Orchestration is not to be separated from composition. It is an important factor in the whole scheme of a work and indeed the medium for which any work is written helps to determine the shape of its themes and their development. We have already mentioned the use that orchestral timbres may be put to in delineating characters in opera, a method which is obviously a by-product of the Wagnerian principle of " Leitmotive ".

CHAPTER XII

THE COMPASSES OF THE INSTRUMENTS. STRING HARMONICS.
FOREIGN NAMES OF INSTRUMENTS WHICH DIFFER FROM OURS

THE INSTRUMENTS are given in the order in which they are found in scores, but before going on to tabulate their compasses a few introductory remarks must be made.

The compasses of the transposing instruments given below are their *written* compasses. The bottom note of any instrument is fixed and virtually unalterable though occasionally composers indicate a lowering of a tone or semitone in the tuning of the lowest string of the violin, viola and 'cello. Examples of this that come to mind are Strauss's temporary tuning down of the second violin's G string to G flat in *Heldenleben,* Tertis's tuning of the C string of the viola down to B flat in the slow movement of his transcription of Elgar's 'cello concerto, and in the domain of chamber music Schumann's direction to the 'cellist to tune his C string down to B flat in his Piano quartet. Kodaly in his unaccompanied 'cello sonata tunes the two lowest strings to B and F sharp and is thus able to get chords that are normally impossible. The double bass is sometimes tuned differently from the usual method by individual players and some are fitted with a fifth string which enables their lower compass to be extended by a third or even a fourth, but by far the majority tune their instruments in the way we show below. In addition to the compasses of the stringed instruments we give their open strings for the sake of completeness.

When we come to the top limits of compass there are in the case of some of the instruments a few higher notes that can be reached by virtuosi. The top notes given below are those attainable by the general run of good orchestral musicians.

The upward compasses of the stringed instruments can be considerably extended by means of harmonics. These are of two kinds, natural and artificial. Natural harmonics are produced by touching the string lightly at a point which will form a node, causing the string to vibrate in fractional parts and thus sound one of its upper partials. On the violin the second, third, fourth, fifth and sixth upper partials can be obtained in this way, the open string providing the fundamental note. Thus from the G string the following harmonics can be produced (the fundamental is numbered 1 and is omitted here):

The string can therefore be made to vibrate in two, three, four, five or six sections by touching the string at the appropriate nodal point. The same series can be obtained from the other three open strings. It is therefore only necessary to transpose the above to correspond with D, A and E as fundamentals to be in possession of all the available natural harmonics of the violin. Some of these will be found to be reduplicated in the different series. The top natural harmonic available on the E string will therefore be the exceedingly high note B one octave above the fifth leger line.

Artificial harmonics are sounded by depressing the string in the normal way with the first finger and touching it with the little finger at a point a fourth above. This causes the stopped string to vibrate in four sections giving the note two octaves above the note produced by the first finger. The depressed note is written as a normal one, the note touched by the fourth finger is designated by a white diamond-shaped symbol. The lowest note obtainable as an artificial harmonic obviously must be:

The highest practicable artificial harmonic is :

To find the natural and artificial harmonics obtainable on the viola the above need only be transposed down a fifth.

On the 'cello the natural harmonics are also the same as those on the violin transposed down a twelfth, but some relatively higher artificial harmonics can be produced up to :

On the double bass natural harmonics are the only kind possible, as the stretch of the fourth is too great for the first and little finger to encompass on one string and this makes artificial harmonics impracticable. Natural harmonics do not come out very clearly on the bottom " E " string and only two are available, the fourth and fifth sounding E and G sharp. On the other strings they are easy to produce and come out clearly. They are of course the same as on the violin if the necessary adjustments of pitch are allowed for, but more upper partials than the five given for the violin are available on the top two strings. Ravel is fond of double bass harmonics (e.g. *Rapsodie Espagnole*) and Sibelius uses them effectively in *Tapiola*.

String harmonics are not used solely or even mainly in order to reach greater altitudes than can be reached by ordinary fingering, in fact many of them are well within the reach of ordinary fingering. They have a special tone-quality, ethereal and elusive, which must be familiar to the reader and it is this which attracts composers.

Rapid passages in harmonics are used in solo violin music of a virtuoso character but in the orchestra these sounds are usually confined to slow or long-held notes. For the sake of completeness it should be added that there are also other ways of producing artificial harmonics which are occasionally used in solo string writing. The method given above is the best for orchestral use. Composers often indicate that they wish a note to be played as a harmonic by writing the required sound with the harmonic sign over it, e.g.:

The method of production is left to the player. Harmonics can be played tremolo.

More information on this subject is given in the larger treatises which give detailed information on the technique of the instruments of the orchestra.

We now give the compasses of the instruments with a few remarks added about each.

THE WOODWIND SECTION

FLUTE :   PICCOLO :

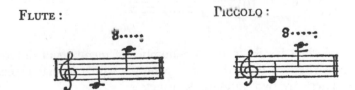

The piccolo sounds an octave higher. Note that it does not possess the low C and C sharp.

The alto (" Bass ") Flute has the same compass as the Flute but sounds a fourth lower. It is in G.

OBOE :   COR ANGLAIS :

The Cor Anglais sounds a fifth lower. Its transposition is therefore the same as that of the Horn in F. The comparatively rare Heckelphone (" Bass Oboe ") has the same written compass as the Cor Anglais but sounds an octave lower instead of a fifth. The extremely high notes of these last two instruments are hardly ever needed, being better in quality and easier to produce on the Oboe. The whole point of their existence is to extend the Oboe tone downwards but they both have very characteristic tone-colours of their own.

The Oboe d'amore, used by Bach and occasionally written for in modern works, lies between the Oboe and Cor Anglais in pitch. It is less heavy and melancholy than the Cor Anglais. Its compass (written) is the same as that given for the Cor Anglais but its transposition is that of an instrument in A, i.e. it sounds a minor third lower than the written notes.

CLARINET :

The Clarinet family includes a number of members of different sizes. They all have the same compass which is that given above. There are two standard Clarinets :

  (1)   in B flat sounding a tone lower.
  (2)   in A sounding a minor third lower.

The Bass Clarinet is now only made in B flat but has an extra key to give the written low E flat so that it can play parts written for the instrument in A. Its part is written in the treble clef and sounds a major ninth lower, i.e. the same as an ordinary B flat clarinet with an octave added on. The rare contrabass Clarinet is also in B flat, sounding two octaves and a tone below the written note. The small Clarinet in E flat sounds a minor third higher and the alto E flat instrument (used in American Symphonic Bands) sounds a major sixth lower like the old E flat horn. The Clarinet in C often used in the Classics is obsolete. The notes from the topmost G upwards are rather screamy and are not much used. The high notes of the Bass Clarinet are not needed unless the line it is playing covers a very wide range of pitch.

The small E flat instrument is sometimes used in the orchestra and is a regular member of the Military Band. It should be mentioned that the bass clef is sometimes used for the Bass and Contrabass Clarinets but players prefer the treble clef because the part can then be read and fingered as it would be on the ordinary standard Clarinet in B flat.

BASSETT-HORN :

This sounds a fifth lower. It was used by Mozart and his contemporaries but fell into disuse in the nineteenth-century probably due to the invention of the bass clarinet. Contemporary composers sometimes use it and it is played when required in eighteenth-century music. It has its own characteristic tone. Not all Clarinet players possess one, and it must come under the head of rare instruments in modern times.

BASSOON: DOUBLE BASSOON:

Three more semitones upward can be reached by expert soloists on the Bassoon, giving a top note of F. The Double Bassoon sounds an octave lower. The top note given for this is a somewhat conservative estimate but the quality of the high notes is not particularly valuable. Some classical works, notably Beethoven's Choral Symphony and Brahms's First Symphony in C minor contain some very athletic and high Double Bassoon writing which is fortunately covered up by the general orchestral sound. I imagine that in these passages the composers wrote " col basso " in the Double Bassoon part and did not realise they were expecting too much of the player as they might have done if they had written the actual notes into the part. There may, however, now be virtuosi who can manage these passages especially if they are able to concentrate mainly on the instrument instead of having to devote most of their time to the normal Bassoon. The Sarrusophone is sometimes used, especially by French composers, instead of the Double Bassoon. Its part is also written an octave higher than the sounds and its bottom note is the same B flat as that of the Double Bassoon. It can also go higher with more ease and comfort up a fifth above the top note we have given for the Double Bassoon, and is said to be generally easier to play and to produce its tone more readily than that instrument. Actually all instruments capable of reaching very low depths of pitch sound very much alike, e.g. Double Bassoon, Contrabass Clarinet and Sarrusophone and even the Tuba on its lowest notes.

THE BRASS SECTION:

HORN:

The standard valve-horn in F sounds a fifth lower. Formerly notes written in the bass clef reversed the transposition and so they would sound a fourth higher. This notation has been used until recent times and some composers still adhere to it even now. In that usage the bottom note would be the low F sharp shown in brackets.

The lowest note of all three-valve brass instruments is a diminished fifth, (or augmented fourth) below the lowest note obtainable when no valves are depressed. This is the written note C for transposing instruments, therefore for them their bottom note is (written) F sharp or G flat. Counting the open position there are seven combinations of valves possible; this accounts for the span of a diminished fifth between the lowest note attainable without valves and the lowest with valves because there are seven semitones in that interval. We know that there are also seven positions of the slide in the case of the trombone. That instrument therefore conforms to the diminished fifth rule also.

TRUMPET:

The standard trumpet is in B flat and sounds a tone lower. We should perhaps mention that jazz players can go a good deal higher than the top C given here. Trumpet parts are often written for C trumpet (non-transposing). The trumpet in D is used for high eighteenth-century parts and also for specially high modern ones. It sounds a tone *higher* than the written note. The Trumpet in A, a modification of the B flat instrument, has dropped out of use. It was really just the B flat Trumpet with a longer shank fitted. This made the intonation of notes obtained by the valves unreliable or difficult to adjust. Parts written for the Trumpet in A are played on the B flat instrument, the player doing the necessary transposition down a semitone.

The Cornet is in B flat and has the same compass as the Trumpet.

TENOR TROMBONE : (in B flat) :

I have given D as the highest note and it would not be very wise to write above that pitch, which is the tenth harmonic in the first position, though first-rate players can play the eleventh and twelfth harmonics (E flat and F). They have to go as high as this in playing some of the classical Alto Trombone parts.

Though the first (closed slide) position gives the B flat series the Tenor Trombone is not a transposing instrument.

Unlike the Horn and Trumpet, Trombones can play the fundamental notes in each position though they are difficult to produce lower than the third position. They are called " Pedal Notes ". We can thus add at least three more notes to those we have given but they do not connect up semitonally to the normal bottom note, E.

Lower fundamentals than these can be coaxed out of the instrument but do not " speak " very readily.

For completeness we should add that the Alto Trombone (now obsolete) was in E flat and its compass was therefore a fourth above that of the tenor instrument.

BASS TROMBONE IN G :

Pedal notes are rarely used though they can be played in the first two or three positions.

The Bass Trombone in F is used a good deal abroad. This has a compass a tone lower than the G Trombone. Some G Trombones are fitted with a mechanical adjunct which can be used to produce the five semitones connecting the low C sharp given above with the first position pedal note G. This would place the C and B of the F Trombone within reach. But the bottom few notes of the Bass Trombone are not very much used, as a lot of breath is needed for them and they are of rather poor or coarse quality.

Experiments have been made with seven-valve mechanism instead of valves, but they were not fruitful and I doubt if they are used anywhere now. I can remember the late Sir Henry Wood using them for a few seasons many years ago. They lacked, I believe, the tone and character of the true Trombone and he soon reverted to the old type.

TUBA (BASS TUBA):

This instrument is fitted with four valves instead of the normal three. The bottom note given is not the lowest written by composers, E natural and E flat at any rate being fairly commonly met with. These notes are good in soft playing but are not capable of much power. It is rare to find a Tuba part that goes as high as the top F given, though Ravel writes up to the G sharp above that in Bydlo in his orchestration of the Moussorgsky Pictures. This solo lies more in the range of the Tenor Tuba.

TENOR TUBA: (EUPHONIUM):

This is an instrument in B flat. When the treble clef notation
(b) is used it sounds a ninth lower like the Bass Clarinet. Notation
(a) is, of course, non-transposing. This is used in Military Bands,
(b) in Brass Bands. Either may be used in the orchestra. Strauss
employs notation (a) in *Don Quixote,* Holst uses (b) in *The
Planets.*

THE SAXOPHONE SECTION:

This is the written compass of the whole family of Saxophones.
The most commonly used in the orchestra is the Alto in E flat.
This sounds a major sixth lower. The Tenor in B flat sounds a
ninth lower. The Alto and Tenor are used in British Military
Bands. There are also the Soprano in B flat sounding a tone
lower, the Baritone in E flat sounding an octave and a major
sixth lower, and the Bass in B flat sounding two octaves and a
tone lower. Others are Sopranino in F sounding a fourth higher,
Tenor in C sounding an octave lower.

The bottom two or three semitones are not very easily produced and are apt to be rather poor in quality except perhaps
on the Alto E flat instrument.

Occasionally Saxophones have been used to play Horn parts in
incomplete orchestras. The Alto E flat or Tenor B flat (or C)
would be suitable as regards compass but they make a poor substitute especially if played in dance-band style with exaggerated
vibrato. Saxophones of all types are used in French Military
Bands and in the American Symphonic or Concert Band two
Altos, a Tenor, a Baritone and a Bass are to be found. The B flat
Bass sometimes shares its part with the Contrabass Clarinet, their
notations, though not their downward compasses, being the same.

THE PERCUSSION:

TIMPANI:

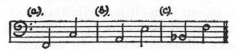

When only two drums are available they will be (a) and (c). The middle drum (b) can be tuned down to G and (a) down to E flat. Top F sharp and G are sometimes written for drum (c). Drums may be fitted with mechanical tuning devices. Two such drums, (a) and (c) should be sufficient. It is more practical to write for three hand-tuned drums, indicating necessary changes of tuning and giving time for them to be made.

Many percussion instruments have no determinate pitch. These include Bass Drum, Cymbals, Side Drum, Triangle, Tambourine, Gong, Woodblock, etc. Their parts are either written on some conventional note in the treble or bass clef or on a single line. Percussion instruments are constantly being added to the list. Some come from the East or from Africa and there is a good crop from Latin-America.

The following instruments of definite pitch and full chromatic compass are usually classified with the percussion section.

GLOCKENSPIEL:

The sounds are two octaves higher.

XYLOPHONE: The same as the Glockenspiel, also sounding two octaves higher.

VIBRAPHONE:

Originally invented in U.S.A. and employed in dance bands, the Vibraphone has recently been taken up by composers of serious music. It sounds as written and both single notes and chords can be played on it. It is in effect a Glockenspiel whose sounds can be sustained (with tremolando effect) by means of an electric or clockwork mechanism.

CELESTA :

This is shown on two staves because music for celesta is written thus, as in piano music. The sounds here are an octave higher.

TUBULAR BELLS :

The above gives approximate limits of pitch. The sound is as written. It is not often that the whole gamut of bells is required. Sometimes only one or two will suffice for a composer's needs, though a peal may be wanted in some festive piece.

THE HARP :

The technique of the harp is described in Chapter V.

The Mandoline has been used in recent works, e.g. Stravinsky's *Agon*. It is also sometimes employed in Opera to give local colour. Its tuning is the same as that of the violin, but each string is reduplicated so that the plectrum with which it is played can produce the tremolando effect characteristic of the instrument.

MANDOLINE :

The notes sound as written.

The Guitar has become a solo instrument capable of much execution and musical expression, and is no longer regarded as exclusively to be connected with Spanish idioms, though naturally it is useful for local colour. Concertos have been written for it in modern times. A Guitar concerto was also written by Hummel.

GUITAR :

THE STRINGS :

The following compasses are given as safe with regard to the upper limits for orchestral playing. They apply to ordinary notes only, not to harmonics which take the instruments up to still higher altitudes. See explanation of natural and artificial harmonics early in this chapter.

o

VIOLIN :   OPEN STRINGS :

VIOLA :   OPEN STRINGS :

VIOLONCELLO :   OPEN STRINGS :

DOUBLE BASS :   OPEN STRINGS :

Sounding an octave lower.

The names of most of the instruments differ very slightly from one another in the languages most frequently encountered in orchestral scores, namely, English, Italian, French and German. But there are some divergences as follows :

BASSOON in Italian is FAGOTTO, in German FAGOTT.
DOUBLE BASSOON in Italian is CONTRAFAGOTTO, in German KONTRAFAGOTT.
HORN in Italian is CORNO, in French COR.
TRUMPET in Italian is TROMBA, plural TROMBE.
TROMBONE in German is POSAUNE.

TIMPANI in French is TIMBALES, in German PAUKEN.
BASS DRUM in Italian is GRAN CASSA, in French GROSSE
    CAISSE, in German GROSSE TROMELL.
CYMBALS in Italian are PIATTI, in German BECKEN.
TAMBOURINE in French is TAMBOUR DE BASQUE, in German
    SCHELLENTROMMEL.
TENOR DRUM in Italian is TAMBURO RULANTE, in French CAISSE
    ROULANTE, in German RUHRTROMMEL.
GONG in all the other three languages is TAM-TAM.
BELLS (TUBULAR) in Italian is CAMPANELLA, in French CLOCHES,
    in German GLOCKEN (distinguish from Glockenspiel).
Americans call the Side Drum the SNARE-DRUM.

The same language should be used all down the score. A mixture of language offends the eye. Italian names are often used by composers of all nationalities; that language is a musical *lingua franca* and Italian musical terms are known to all musicians. There is much to be said therefore for listing the instruments under their Italian names.

BIBLIOGRAPHY

BERLIOZ, HECTOR

Traité d'instrumentation.
Eng. trans. Novello.

CARSE, ADAM

The History of Orchestration.
Kegan Paul & Co.

The Orchestra in the XVIIIth Century.
W. Heffer & Sons Ltd., Cambridge.

The Orchestra from Beethoven to Berlioz.
W. Heffer & Sons Ltd., Cambridge.

FORSYTH, CECIL

Orchestration.
MacMillan & Co. Ltd.

GEVAERT, F. A.

Traité general d'instrumentation.
Paris, 1885.

JACOB, GORDON

Orchestral Technique.
Oxford University Press.

How to Read a Score.
Boosey & Hawkes Ltd.

PISTON, WALTER

Orchestration.
Victor Gollancz Ltd. (Eng. edn.)

213

BIBLIOGRAPHY

PROUT, EBENEZER — *The Orchestra,* Vols. 1 and 2.
Augener Ltd.
Orchestration (Primer).
Novello & Co. Ltd.

RIMSKY-KORSAKOV — *Principes d'Orchestration*
Edition Russe de Musique.

(An English translation has been published in New York.)

WIDOR, C. M. — *The Technique of the Modern Orchestra.*
Joseph Williams.
(Appendix to the Revised edition, 1946, by Gordon Jacob.)

INDEX

215